Grand Prêtre

Simple Prêtre

Arche d'Alliance

Autel des Holocaustes

Autel du Parfum

Camp d'Israel autour du Tabernacle

Occident

Parvis et Tabernacle

Chandelier d'Or

EXPLORE THE TABERNACLE OF MOSES
IN THE LIGHT OF THE SON

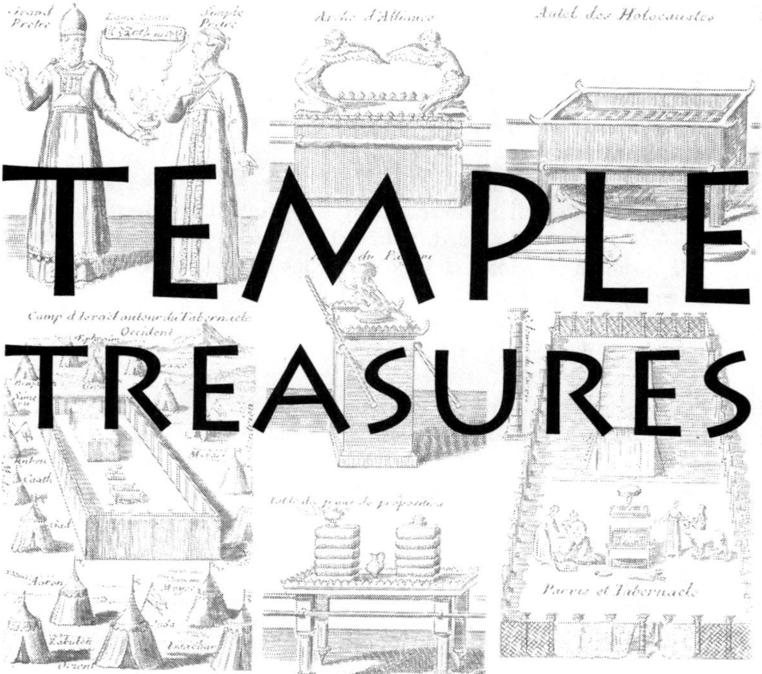

TEMPLE TREASURES

STEVEN FUSON

Alachua, Florida 32615

Bridge-Logos
Alachua, FL 32615 USA

Temple Treasures
by Steve Fuson

Printed in the United States of America.

Library of Congress Catalog Card Number: 2010933317
International Standard Book Number: 978-0-88270-419-7

Scripture quotations: See Appendix.

G352.316.N.m1010.35220

DEDICATION

This book is dedicated to my beloved mother and father. Their lives testify to the transforming power of the love and the light of the indwelling Christ.

Contents

Preface: An Exploration of the Temple of God. ix
Introduction: Behold the Temple Treasures! xiii

Part One: The Court 1
The Gate: Faith 3
The Brazen Altar: Spiritual Sacrifices 15
The Laver: Examination and Cleansing 27
Aaron's Garments: The Lord, Our Righteousness 37

Part Two: The Holy Place 49
First Veil: Divine Government 51
The Showbread: Teachings of Truth 63
The Golden Candlestick: Divine Illumination 75
The Golden Altar: Prayer and Praise 87

Part Three: The Holy of Holies 97
The Inner Veil: Open Heavens 99
The Golden Ark: God's Heart in Man 105
The Cherubim: Spirit Baptism 117

The Mercy Seat: Atonement 133
The Two Tablets of Stone: Divine Nature 143
The Hidden Manna: Revelation 153
Aaron's Rod: Authority. 171

Conclusion: Temple Insight 189
Appendix: Bible Translations 197

An Exploration of the Temple of God

Using This Book to Discover Your Temple Treasures

This book is an exploration of the wondrous Temple not made by human hands. The Bible says that we—God's people—are the Temples of the living God. So in a very real sense we are challenged to explore the Temple in which God has chosen to dwell.

The Bible explains how Moses was with God for forty days on Mount Sinai. During this time God gave Moses very specific instructions on how to construct the Tabernacle in the wilderness. In strict obedience to God's instructions, Moses established the court, the Holy Place, and the Holy of Holies. The Bible refers to God's instructions as *the pattern* of the Tabernacle. Our exploration begins with the study of this ancient pattern.

We carefully adhere to the biblical blueprint—or pattern—in our spiritual exploration of the Temple. The Bible is our guide each step of the way.

The Bible describes God's people as earthen vessels who contain spiritual treasures. The goal of our exploration is to discover these Temple treasures. We will use this term, *Temple treasures*, to identify our inheritance in Jesus Christ. The Son of God dwells in our hearts by faith, and in Him we possess all the riches of the Kingdom of Heaven.

Features to Help the Reader:

In accordance to the pattern given to Moses, this book explores the court, the Holy Place, and the Holy of Holies in sequential order. Each aspect of the overall pattern is presented with the following helpful features:

Name

Each aspect of the pattern is named. For instance, the first aspect of the pattern is *The Gate of the Court.* The name provides a convenient reference point, which is based on Scripture.

Key Word

Each aspect of the pattern is ascribed a key word. The key word, a distillation of many relevant Scriptures, conveys the spiritual essence of the aspect under consideration. For instance, the Gate of the Court is ascribed the key word, *Faith.*

Significance

Each aspect of the pattern is explained in terms of its spiritual significance. This is a synopsis consisting of three or four sentences. The significance, combined with the key word, begins the discovery of a treasure of incomparable value.

Supportive Scriptures

This is a short list of Bible verses that provides support for the aspect of the pattern under consideration. These verses are fully quoted for the reader's edification. Note on Bible quotations: All biblical quotations are from the New King James Version, unless otherwise specified.

Physical Description

Each aspect of the pattern is described in physical terms, as it would have looked in Moses' day. It is helpful to create this visual image. The physical pattern becomes a symbol of great spiritual promise.

Spiritual Application

The physical aspects of the pattern are applied spiritually to the lives of God's people. In essence, the physical attributes of the historic Tabernacle built by Moses become spiritual attributes of those who dwell in the Temple of Jesus Christ.

Rhyming Couplets

The study of each aspect concludes with a rhyming couplet, which reflects on the Temple treasure being explored. The couplets help the reader summarize the study.

Author's Prayer for the Reader

DEAR HEAVENLY FATHER,
ANOINT THE READER WITH THE SPIRIT OF UNDERSTANDING
IN THIS EXPLORATION OF YOUR HOLY TEMPLE.
LET THE READER DISCOVER THE ABUNDANCE OF SPIRITUAL
TREASURE YOU HAVE PREPARED FOR YOUR PEOPLE.
WE THANK YOU FOR THE VICTORY, FATHER,
IN THE NAME OF YOUR SON, JESUS.
AMEN.

BEHOLD THE TEMPLE TREASURES!

THIS PRECIOUS TREASURE—THIS LIGHT AND POWER THAT NOW SHINE WITHIN US—IS HELD IN A PERISHABLE CONTAINER, THAT IS, IN OUR WEAK BODIES. EVERYONE CAN SEE THAT THE GLORIOUS POWER WITHIN MUST BE FROM GOD AND IS NOT OUR OWN.
2 CORINTHIANS 4:7, TLB

Jesus: The Temple of His Body

The discovery of our Temple treasures begins with our Savior, Jesus Christ. He was the perfect embodiment of the Temple during His earthly ministry, and He showed forth remarkable spiritual treasures. Jesus referred to Himself as the Temple in the following manner:

> *Jesus answered and said to them, "Destroy this temple, and in three days I will raise it up." Then the Jews said, "It has taken forty-six years to build this temple, and will You raise it up in three days?" But He was speaking of the temple of His body.* JOHN 2:19-21

The religious leaders of Jesus' day were obsessed with the physical edifice that had taken nearly a half-century to construct. Historical records indicate that the Temple in

Jerusalem was architecturally impressive in both size and design. The pride of the religious leaders in their sacred Temple was understandable. Indeed, their religious tradition had always focused on the physical Temple since the time of Moses.

Jesus' statements caught the religious leadership off-guard when He said, "*Destroy this temple...*" They assumed He was referring to their sacred Temple. However, "*...He was speaking of the temple of His body.*" He was very much aware of the Father's plan that He—the Son—would be crucified at the hands of these same religious leaders, and that He would be resurrected by the Father on the third day.

The Son made the startling assertion that His body—a physical tabernacle of flesh and blood—was the Temple of God. This truth resonates in the heart of every believer who grasps its impact on their personal life. However, the religious leaders of Israel, bound by tradition and protocol, could not grasp the spiritual implications of such a profoundly life-changing concept.

Jesus transferred the focus from the traditional religious building—a Temple made by human hands—to the Temple of His body. His ministry, crucifixion, Resurrection, and glorification would forever establish the Temple *not* made by hands. In the person of the Savior the focus was dramatically shifted from a material religious edifice to the lives of God's people. It was revealed that God's people were the collective *Body of Christ* and that His Spirit and Word wondrously dwelt within the hearts of all believers.

The religious hierarchy of Israel misunderstood Jesus. Their allegiance was to the Old Covenant of Law instituted by Moses, whereas Jesus inaugurated a New Covenant of grace and truth. "*For the law was given through Moses, but grace and truth came through Jesus Christ*" (John 1:17). The Old Covenant of Law placed all emphasis upon the physical Tabernacle with its exclusive priesthood headed up by Aaron. We will refer to the priesthood that developed under Aaron as the Aaronic Order.

The physical Tabernacle built by Moses we will refer to as the Mosaic Tabernacle.

Jesus was confronted by the timeworn traditionalists who were loyal to the Old Law Covenant. Their focus on the material Temple in Jerusalem caused them to resent, to persecute, and ultimately to crucify the Son of God. They continually accused Jesus from the written Law of the Old Testament—the Old Covenant. In the face of this hostility, Jesus was constrained to speak the following truth:

> *"I say to you that in this place there is One greater than the temple."* MATTHEW 12:6

This offended the religious authorities. To them the material Temple of mortar and stone was the end result of the Mosaic Tabernacle in the wilderness. Theirs was an ancient tradition based on a sacred building, an exclusive priesthood decked in formal priestly attire, a strict ritualistic code, and the sacrifice of animals for the purpose of atonement. Jesus stood in their midst as the living Temple of God—as one who was far greater than their sacred earthly Temple. Yet they did not recognize or honor Him as the Temple.

The Savior did not fit the religious mold established in the minds of the religious leaders. He did not meet their expectations of the Messiah—the Anointed One—even though He *was* the Messiah. Consider a few points of difference:

- The Aaronic Order was limited to men from the tribe of Levi, whereas Jesus was from the tribe of Judah.
- The priests of the Aaronic Order clothed themselves in elaborate priestly garb, whereas Jesus wore the clothes of the common people.
- The religious hierarchy expected the Messiah to restore Israel to its former greatness as a human kingdom, whereas Jesus offered a kingdom not of this world.

- The religious hierarchy, prideful of their elite status, disdained the poor, whereas Jesus lived among the common folk and ministered to their needs with compassion.
- The Aaronic Order was an insiders' club that militantly defended their turf, whereas Jesus opened the doors of the kingdom to all mankind.
- The Aaronic Order was obsessed with the ritualistic slaughter of animals to bring temporary remission of sin, whereas Jesus established the Melchizedek Order and through His singular death on the Cross brought remission of sin to all of humanity for all time.
- Last, but certainly not least, the religious hierarchy placed all of their focus, energy, effort, and devotion on the material, physical Temple. In sharp contrast, Jesus offered himself as the personal manifestation of the Father's kingdom, power, and glory.

We magnify the Son of God in light of these glorious transformations, which He inaugurated. In fulfilling the Old, He established the New.

Old Kingdom: Israel	New Kingdom: Kingdom of Heaven
Old Covenant: Law	New Covenant: Grace and Truth
Old Order: Aaronic	New Order: Melchizedek
Old Priesthood: Levitical	New Priesthood: A Royal Priesthood of All Believers
Old Temple: Mosaic	New Temple: The Temple of His Body

Jesus taught that His purpose was to fulfill the Law, not to destroy it. It is essential that we recognize the Mosaic Tabernacle as the pattern that Jesus perfectly fulfilled. The following verses help support the concept that Jesus was indeed the Temple of God.

When the Messiah arrived, high priest of the superior things of this new covenant, he bypassed the old tent and its trappings in this created world and went straight into heaven's "tent"—the true Holy Place—once and for all. He also bypassed the sacrifices consisting of goat and calf blood, instead using his own blood as the price to set us free once and for all. HEBREWS 9:11-12, MSG

For Christ has entered into heaven itself, to appear now before God as our Friend. It was not in the earthly place of worship that he did this, for that was merely a copy of the real temple in heaven.... He came once for all, at the end of the age [of Law], to put away the power of sin forever by dying for us. HEBREWS 9:24, 26, TLB

When we *uphold* our Savior as the Temple of God, we will *behold* our own Temple inheritance in Him.

Now We Are the Temple of God

The New Testament declares with absolute clarity that everyone who receives the Son by faith is a Temple of God.

Surely you know that you are God's temple, and that God's Spirit lives in you! 1 CORINTHIANS 3:16, TEV

Some translations present this verse as a question: *Don't you realize that you are the temple of God and that His Spirit lives in you?* Our affirmative answer to this question opens to us the Temple treasures. Always keep in mind that the Mosaic Tabernacle did not consist of an empty court and vacant holy places. Quite the contrary. The Mosaic Tabernacle presented an intricate *pattern*—a symbolic design—consisting of special furnishings made of cloth, animal skins, acacia wood, brass, silver, and gold. Every furnishing, every item, and every aspect holds vast spiritual riches of meaning. These treasures await our exploration.

> *Have you forgotten that your body is the temple of the Holy Spirit, who lives in you, and is God's gift to you, and that you are not the owner of your own body? You have been bought, and at what a price! Therefore bring glory to God in your body.* 1 CORINTHIANS 6:19-20, PH

The above Bible verse acknowledges that it is possible to forget our inheritance as the Temple of God. The everyday cares and concerns of life can cloud our perception of the fact that God's Spirit indwells these earthen vessels with spiritual abundance. It is time to remember. It is time to consider our true inheritance in Christ. It is time to discover the treasures promised us through the death and Resurrection of the Son.

> *For you are the temple of the living God. As God has said: "I will dwell in them and walk among them. I will be their God, and they shall be My people.... Come out from among them and be separate," says the LORD. "Do not touch what is unclean, and I will receive you. I will be a Father to you, and you shall be My sons and daughters," says the LORD Almighty.* 2 CORINTHIANS 6:16-18

These Scriptures state the noble intentions of a loving Father. He embraces us as His Temple, His people, and His own sons and daughters. This is our magnificent heritage in the Son.

Explore the Pattern

The Bible makes it clear that we are the Temples of the living God. This is one of the key insights of the gospel, or the good news, of Jesus Christ. This insight, as wonderful as it is, should awaken our interest in the original pattern of the earthly

Temple. When we consider that the pattern of the Temple was revealed directly by God to Moses, we should not be satisfied until we can answer these questions: What does the pattern mean in spiritual terms? How do I apply the pattern to my spiritual walk in God?

Please take note of the vital importance placed upon the pattern of the Temple in the Old Testament:

> *And let them* [Israel] *make Me a sanctuary, that I may dwell among them. According to all that I show you* [Moses], *that is, the* ***pattern of the tabernacle and the pattern of all its furnishings, just so you shall make it.*** EXODUS 25:8-9, EMPHASIS ADDED

> *And see to it that you make them* ***according to the pattern*** *which was shown you on the mountain.* EXODUS 25:40, EMPHASIS ADDED

> *And you shall raise up the tabernacle* ***according to its pattern*** *which you were shown on the mountain.* EXODUS 26:30, EMPHASIS ADDED

> *Thus all the work of the tabernacle of the tent of meeting was finished. And the children of Israel did* ***according to all that the LORD had commanded Moses; so they did.*** EXODUS 39:32, EMPHASIS ADDED

The same strong emphasis upon the pattern of the Temple is given in the New Testament, as follows:

> *Our fathers had the tabernacle of witness in the wilderness, as He appointed, instructing Moses to make it* ***according to the pattern*** *that he had seen.* ACTS 7:44, EMPHASIS ADDED

> *These men* [the Aaronic priesthood under Moses] *are serving what is only a pattern or reproduction of things that exist in Heaven. (Moses, you will remember, when he was going to construct the tabernacle, was cautioned by God in these words: See that you make all things* ***according to the pattern*** *showed thee in the mount).*
> HEBREWS 8:5, PH, EMPHASIS ADDED

Moses constructed the Tabernacle in strict accordance to the pattern he received from God. In this book we will carefully consider each aspect of the Mosaic Tabernacle in the light of the New Testament. We will study the pattern, and its correspondent spiritual applications, with all due reverence and awe. For the pattern of the Mosaic Tabernacle comes to us as a gift from our loving Father, who wants us to know what it means to be the Temple of the living God.

The Old Testament provides the pattern, but the New Testament provides the spiritual reality. We can view the Old Covenant of Law as a symbolic pattern that has no life within itself. The New Covenant of grace and truth, however, reveals the everlasting life of the Son in the hearts of His people.

God spoke the following words through the prophet Ezekiel: "*...shew the house to the house...*" (Ezekiel 43:10, KJV). This unusual phrase may seem a little obscure at first, yet it conveys the essence of this book. Please consider. *Show the house to the house* means to show the Temple treasures to God's people. Show the majesty of the Temple inheritance to the people who comprise the house of the Lord. Show the spiritual meaning of the house, or Temple, to the collective household of faith. Show the Temple to the Temple.

In this book God issues a challenge to His people to explore their Temple treasures. Study the blueprint of the house you inhabit spiritually. Discover the Temple of the Son, the indwelling Christ "*...in whom are hidden all the treasures of wisdom and knowledge*" (Colossians 2:3).

We will begin our exploration of hidden treasure as we approach the gate of the court with great anticipation.

PART ONE

The Court

How lovely is Your tabernacle, O Lord of hosts! My soul longs, yes, even faints for the courts of the Lord; my heart and my flesh cry out for the living God. For a day in Your courts is better than a thousand. I would rather be a doorkeeper in the house of my God than dwell in the tents of wickedness. For the Lord God is a sun and shield; the Lord will give grace and glory; no good thing will He withhold from those who walk uprightly. O Lord of hosts, blessed is the man who trusts in You!

Psalm 84:1-2; 10-12

Those who are planted in the house of the Lord shall flourish in the courts of our God. They shall still bear fruit in old age; they shall be fresh and flourishing, to declare that the Lord is upright; He is my rock, and there is no unrighteousness in Him.

Psalm 92:13-15

THE GATE

Key Word: Faith

Significance

The gate signifies faith in Jesus Christ as the firstborn Son of God. It is this precious, elemental experience of faith in the Anointed One as our Savior that brings new birth into the Kingdom of God. The gate of faith provides entrance into the court of the Lord's house.

Supportive Scriptures

Jesus said to them again, "Most assuredly, I say to you, I am the door of the sheep.... I am the door. If anyone enters by Me, he will be saved, and will go in and out and find pasture." JOHN 10:7, 9

Jesus said to him, "I am the way, the truth, and the life. No one comes to the Father except through Me." JOHN 14:6

Your way, O God, is in the sanctuary; who is so great a God as our God? PSALM 77:13

I have chosen the way of truth.... Teach me, O LORD, the way of the Your statutes, and I shall keep it to the end. PSALM 119:30, 33

I am not ashamed of the gospel of Christ, for it is the power of God to salvation for everyone who believes. ROMANS 1:16

Whoever believes that Jesus is the Christ is born of God.... He who believes in the Son of God has the witness in himself; he who does not believe God has made Him a liar, because he has not believed the testimony that God has given of His Son. And this is the testimony: that God has given us eternal life, and this life is in His Son. 1 JOHN 5:1; 10-11

Physical Description

The gate into the court consisted of the same beautiful linen curtains that encompassed the entire court, except for one exquisite detail. That is, the gate curtain was not white. Instead, it was quite striking in its bold display of royal colors—an intricate pattern of blue, purple, and scarlet that would billow softly in the wilderness breeze. The brilliant colors of the hand-stitched, fine-twined linen curtains were radiant in the sunlight.

The hanging for ***the gate of the court*** *was needlework, of blue, and purple, and scarlet, and fine twined linen: and twenty cubits* [thirty feet] *was the length, and the height in the breadth was five cubits* [seven-and-one-half feet], *answerable* [similar] *to the hangings of the court.* EXODUS 38:18, KJV, EMPHASIS ADDED

A cubit was approximately eighteen inches. An individual, standing in front of the gate, could not see over the top of the curtain. However, a person standing on a nearby hillside could look down upon the open court. The Tabernacle, situated in the center of the court, was covered.

It is interesting to note the size of the court compared to the Tabernacle. The court measured seventy-five feet in width by one hundred fifty feet in length (see Exodus 27:18). The Tabernacle, determined from scriptural data, measured approximately eighteen feet in width by forty-five feet in length (see Exodus 26:15-25). Therefore, the total area of the court was over twelve times larger than the Tabernacle. The court's expansive size takes on strong symbolic meaning once we progress into our Temple treasures.

The gate was on the east end of the court. Therefore the gate received the first rays of the rising morning sun—an important symbolic reminder of the Savior's Resurrection morning and our personal resurrection in Him.

There were ten pillars that supported the full span of the eastern court curtain. The four middle pillars supported the gate curtain proper, while the outermost pillars on either side of the gate carried the curtain to each corner. All pillars that encompassed the court, including the pillars of the gate, were made of brass and were set upon sockets of brass.

The Bible refers to the court curtain as *hangings.* These cloth hangings, or individual curtains, were carried on silver fillets, or fence rails, which connected the pillars. The curtains were attached to the fillets with silver hooks. Hooks were also used to attach the curtains to each pillar around the entire court. However, the curtains at the eastern gate were not connected to their pillars so that the priests could simply part the curtains in order to enter the court. In the time of Moses, only Aaron and his sons had access into the gate of the court. We refer to this priestly order under the Law as the Aaronic Order.

Keep in mind that the children of God through faith in the Son are *a priesthood of all believers.* Under the New Covenant of grace and truth, all who believe in the Son of God have indeed entered into the court. That is to say, the entire family of God now enters the gate of faith instead of an officially appointed priesthood. The spiritual reality of grace far exceeds the type-and-shadow of the Law. As we study our Temple treasures, we will learn this principle: The physical court and Tabernacle under the Law Covenant were mere shadows compared to the marvelous light revealed in the Son.

The gate is referred to in these terms:

- the gate of the court (Exodus 27:16)
- the court gate (Exodus 38:15)
- the door of the gate of the court (Numbers 4:26)
- the curtain for the door of the court (Numbers 3:26, KJV)

Quite simply, the gate was the way into the court, and the court was the way into the Tabernacle, which consisted of the Holy Place and the Holy of Holies. Symbolically, then, the gate held tremendous significance. Today we can have spiritual understanding by which we apply the meaning of the gate to the life of every believer.

Spiritual Application

The gate is faith in the Son of God. It is the inner spiritual awakening in the human soul by which one experiences new life and hope in Christ. The Apostle Peter experienced the gate of faith when he openly confessed to the Savior, "*You are the Christ, the Son of the living God*" (Matthew 16:16). When Jesus restored the sight of a man who was born blind, the man confessed, "*'Lord, I believe!' And he worshipped Him*" (John 9:38). Each of the apostles and disciples experienced the transformational power of faith in the Savior. "*Jesus... manifested forth his glory; and his disciples believed on him*" (John 2:11, KJV).

Belief in the Savior floods the heart of every newborn child of God with the comfort and joy of the Holy Spirit. Belief in the Savior provides our entrance into eternal fellowship with the Father and Son. The Savior stated it so beautifully: "*For God* [the Father] *so loved the world that He gave His only begotten Son, that whoever believes in Him should not perish but have everlasting life*" (John 3:16).

The entrance of faith into the human heart is the greatest of all spiritual gifts. No amount of human religious works can earn faith. The fact that the Savior imparts the free gift of faith is as much of a miracle as healing the sick, restoring blind eyes and deaf ears, and even raising the dead back to life. It is this elemental faith in the Son that translates the human soul out of carnal darkness into spiritual light. *"For by grace you have been saved through faith, and that not of yourselves:* ***it is the gift of God,*** *not of works, lest anyone should boast"* (Ephesians 2:8-9, emphasis added). The gift of faith opens up the entire court and Temple to the believer.

It is all by grace and not according to Law. The Old Covenant of Law was fulfilled and superceded by the New Covenant of grace and truth. The Tabernacle built by Moses under the Law Covenant was a physical pattern—a symbol—of profound spiritual realities. The physical aspects of the Mosaic Tabernacle were merely types, shadows, and symbols of the spiritual Temple established by grace through faith in every soul who believes in the Son. There is no entrance into the spiritual Temple outside of faith in Jesus the Christ, the Anointed Savior.

> *Without faith it is impossible to please Him, for he who comes to God must believe that He is, and that He is a rewarder of those who diligently seek Him.* HEBREWS 11:6

Entrance through the gate of faith offers great reward. The rich treasures of both the court and the Tabernacle are available only when one passes through the gate. This is the first essential requirement: believe in the Son of God. To be quickened and awakened in one's soul by the gift of faith opens the gate into the beautiful court of the Lord's house.

Many are the Scriptures that can be applied to the gate of faith. Keep in mind that the gate consisted of several curtains and therefore it is sometimes referred to in the plural form *gates.*

> ***Open to me the gates of righteousness;*** *I will go through them, and I will praise the* LORD. ***This is the gate of the*** ***LORD,*** *through which the righteous shall enter.* PSALM 118:19-20, EMPHASIS ADDED

Faith is the gate of the Lord, and in our new birth into Him we experience His righteousness for the first time. His righteousness overwhelms our humanness. In this new spiritual reality we wonderfully discover that we are heirs of the forgiveness, acceptance, and love of God our Father.

Jesus gave explicit instruction to all who desire to receive their true inheritance in God:

> *Enter by the narrow gate....* MATTHEW 7:13

> *Strive to enter through the narrow gate....* LUKE 13:24

Thousands of precious souls entered the gate of faith on the Day of Pentecost, two thousand years ago. Many of these were Israelites who had previously believed in Jehovah, the God of the Old Testament. But it was not enough to believe only in God, for God sent His Son to be the Savior of the world. That is why the Savior counseled the Jewish people: "*You believe in God, believe also in Me*" (John 14:1). The New Covenant of grace and truth opened wide the doors for fellowship with both the Father and the Son. It is a very real and unavoidable principle: The Son is the gateway to the Father. Every page of the New Testament is replete with the revelation that the Son reveals the Father.

The Spirit of God moved upon the prophets of the Old Testament to inspire them to write His Word concerning ultimate faith in His Son. One of the strengths of Old Testament prophecy is its innate ability to bring blessing and inspiration both to those under Law and those under grace. The people of that historic timeframe celebrated a natural gate, court, and

Tabernacle. Today we read the same inspired Word and celebrate its application to the spiritual gate, court, and Tabernacle, which exists within God's people. This is an awesome truth, and we must never let it slip from our minds. *The people of God are His Temple.* Hearken to the voice of the Spirit in the reading of these ancient prophetic words:

> ***Go through, go through the gates! Prepare the way for the people;*** *build up, build up the highway! Take out the stones, lift up a banner for the peoples!* ***And they shall call them The Holy People, The Redeemed of the LORD.*** ISAIAH 62:10, 12, EMPHASIS ADDED

The above Scripture certainly conveyed good tidings to those under the consciousness of the Old Covenant of Law, but how much more perfectly do these words bless those under the consciousness of grace and truth? The Old Testament, when read with a Law-consciousness, provides a shadow of good things to come. The same Old Testament Scriptures, when read with a consciousness of grace and truth, provide the true light. The shadows of symbolic language yield the mind of Christ, which inspired the Scriptures. The Old Testament is the New Testament concealed. The New Testament is the Old Testament revealed.

Faith in the Son: It is the gate and it is the way of the Lord's redeemed people. The universal call to humanity echoes down through the corridors of all ages: Go through the gates of faith!

> ***Open the gates,*** *that the righteous nation which keeps the truth may enter in.* ISAIAH 26:2, EMPHASIS ADDED

The people of Israel received many benefits and blessings because they honored the Covenant of Law with its natural Tabernacle. Infinitely more so today are a people and a nation blessed who have opened and entered the gates of faith to believe in the Son and to keep His truth.

Faith in the Son brings joy to the heart. Once the gate of faith is established in our hearts, it becomes foundational in all that we think, say, or do. On a daily basis we approach God with uplifted hearts full of joyfulness, thanksgiving, and praise. It is a perpetual positive attitude that eternally springs up from the inner gift of faith. This inner condition of joy and thanksgiving was described by the Apostle Peter as "*...joy unspeakable and full of glory*" (1 Peter 1:8, KJV). It manifests in diverse ways. Sometimes the joy manifests in outward, vocal demonstration. Often it flows silently, peacefully within one's soul. Psalm 100 captures this attitude of joy and gladness that simply overflows in each human soul that is in union with God and His purposes. "*...We are His people and the sheep of His pasture. Enter into His gates with thanksgiving, and into His courts with praise. Be thankful to Him, and bless His name*" (Psalm 100:3-4).

God's people are learning this secret of thanksgiving and praise as it applies to both collective and personal worship. This is an invaluable lesson: The gift of faith prospers and finds fullest expression in the presence of joy and gladness.

Faith in the Son is the inheritance of all men and nations. It is the purpose of God that the Temple treasures are revealed in and through mankind. The revelation of the Temple of God in men and women living today will impact our entire planet. God has appointed this present millennium as the timeframe in which the Temple will be fully revealed and restored. The brilliance of this revelation of the Temple will eventually result in a universal willingness to enter the gate of faith.

Ultimately, the people of all nations will recognize faith in the Son as the way of deliverance and healing. Every knee shall bow and every tongue shall confess that Jesus Christ is Lord to the glory of God the Father. Faith in the Son will open the heart of every man, woman, and child to receive the good news of the Kingdom of Heaven. The good news of God's Kingdom will supplant the bad news of earthly despair and death. It is good news that the way of deliverance has only begun to open wide its doors both now and for the ages yet to come.

The following verses testify to the purpose of the ages that the Father has established in the Son.

> *Therefore* ***your gates shall be open continually****; they shall not be shut day or night,* ***that men may bring to you the wealth of the Gentiles*** *[nations],* ***and their kings*** [leaders] ***in procession.*** ISAIAH 60:11, EMPHASIS ADDED

> *...you shall* ***call your walls Salvation, and your gates Praise.*** ISAIAH 60:18, EMPHASIS ADDED

The ancient Israelite, gazing upon the white linen court curtain with its gate of royal colors, never perceived its true beauty and glory in the Spirit. He was not able at that time to internalize its symbolic essence. But thanks be to the Father and Son, now we understand that the walls of salvation and gates of praise dwell in mankind by faith.

Pause to consider this glorious liberty. Humans make religious walls to keep people out or to hold people in confinement. God replaces these man-made religious walls with walls of salvation—the free gift of salvation through faith. All we need to enter the walls of salvation is praise. We praise the Father for giving us His Son, and we praise the Son for revealing to us the Father.

Our understanding of the term *gate* is a master key that unlocks the meaning of many Scriptures. Another key term—*way*—also makes direct reference to the gift of faith. Jesus referred to Himself as *the way.* The import of the following statement by the Son has never wavered: "*I am the way, the truth, and the life*" (John 14:6). The term *way* was often applied to the disciples in the virgin Church. (We will use this term, virgin Church, in reference to the original called-out disciples as described in the Book of Acts.) Saul of Tarsus, a carnal man dedicated to the Old Covenant of Law, viciously hunted down those who walked in *the Way* of salvation.

> *Then Saul, still breathing threats and murder against the disciples of the Lord, went to the high priest and asked letters from him to the synagogues of Damascus, so that if he found* ***any who were of the Way****, whether men or women, he might bring them bound to Jerusalem.* ACTS 9:1-2, EMPHASIS ADDED

> *I* [Saul] *persecuted* ***this Way*** *to the death, binding and delivering into prisons both men and women.* ACTS 22:4, EMPHASIS ADDED

In one of the most remarkable accounts of personal transformation, Saul, persecutor of the Way, became Paul, its greatest advocate. Prior to his change of heart, Saul (meaning *big one*) misunderstood those in the Way to be enemies of the Old Testament of Law with its physical Temple, animal sacrifices, rituals, rites, and holy days. Only after he recognized the Savior by faith did Paul (meaning *little one*) realize that Jesus fulfilled the Law through the Spirit of resurrection life. Paul came to understand that the spiritual reality far exceeded the dead letter code.

Paul met with the resurrected Son face-to-face, and Paul believed in Him. Paul's belief produced inner transformation. Paul's faith in the Son was the way, or the gate, into the spiritual court of the spiritual Temple. Paul's calling as a special vessel of the Lord did not change the fact that he first had to believe. In this elemental faith he was no different from any other believer.

Isaiah the Prophet had foretold of John the Baptist: *"The voice of one crying in the wilderness: 'Prepare the way of the* L*ORD; make straight in the desert a highway for our God'"* (Isaiah 40:3). John the Baptist was anointed of God to direct the people of Israel to believe in the coming Messiah. John emphatically commanded the people to repent, or to change their minds, in preparation to believe in the Son. The dynamics of spiritual transition were in the air. A change in Covenant was in order. The long-awaited Messiah—the Anointed One—was now present among humanity. He was much more than the gate of faith, or the way; indeed, He was the perfect embodiment of the fullness of the Temple of God. Yet, the first principal requirement for the people was to believe in Him. Faith in Him was *the Way of the Lord.* The people were to leave a wilderness condition of dead letter law and tradition to enter the New Covenant founded in the Son.

The following Scriptures again illustrate the promise of salvation that was reserved for the appearance of the anointed Savior. Each of these Scriptures provides a direct reference to faith in the Son.

> ***This is the way,*** *walk in it.* ISAIAH 30:21, EMPHASIS ADDED

> *And* ***an highway*** *shall be there, and* ***a way,*** *and it shall be called* ***The way of holiness....*** ISAIAH 35:8. KJV, EMPHASIS ADDED

> *He who keeps instruction is in* ***the way of life....*** PROVERBS 10:17, EMPHASIS ADDED

> *In* ***the way of righteousness*** *is life, and in its pathway there is no death.* PROVERBS 12:28, EMPHASIS ADDED

> *For You will light my lamp; the LORD my God will enlighten my darkness.... As for God,* ***His way is perfect;*** *the word of the LORD is proven....* PSALM 18:28, 30, EMPHASIS ADDED

Each child of God experiences that initial moment of living faith in the Son of God. Once experienced, the gift of faith never leaves nor forsakes, but it is continually refreshed and experienced anew. It is also the glory of God to impart His faith as a foundational divine principle that elevates both our character and our consciousness. In other words, the gate of faith is not just a momentary experience in God. It is also a divine principle that is written by the Spirit into the character of every believer.

The principle of faith is a stable and steadfast companion throughout the ups and downs of human life. It weathers the storms of adversity. It is an eternal principle, which does not fluctuate according to our moods and emotions.

Therefore we can conclude that personal, elemental faith in the Son of God expresses itself as both experience and principle. Experience in God, combined with divine principle, makes a great team. Throughout our study of the Temple treasures, we will learn that both experience and principle highlight each vessel in the court and the Tabernacle. We must experience the reality of each Temple vessel, yet we must also learn to be mature practitioners of the principles of the kingdom.

I've entered the gate through faith in the Son.
Temple treasures await; for them I now run.

THE BRAZEN ALTAR

Key Words: Spiritual Sacrifices

Significance

The brazen altar signifies the Savior's death on the Cross. The blood of sacrificial animals, utilized under the Old Covenant of Law to atone for sin, established the pattern: Without the shedding of blood there was no remission of sin. The Savior's willing sacrifice upon the Cross fulfilled the pattern through the impartation of eternal redemption, and now we offer up spiritual sacrifices acceptable in Christ Jesus.

Supportive Scriptures

> *Walk in love, as Christ also has loved us and given Himself for us, an offering and a sacrifice to God for a sweet-smelling aroma.* EPHESIANS 5:2

> *Who* [Christ] *does not need daily, as those high priests* [under the Law], *to offer up sacrifices, first for His own sins and then for the people's, for this He did once for all when He offered up Himself.* HEBREWS 7:27

> *If the blood of bulls and goats and the ashes of a heifer, sprinkling the unclean, sanctifies for the purifying of the flesh, how much more shall the blood of Christ, who*

through the eternal Spirit offered Himself without spot to God.... HEBREWS 9:13-14

I desire mercy and not [animal] *sacrifice.* MATTHEW 9:13; 12:7

To Him who loved us and washed us from our sins in His own blood, and has made us kings and priests to His God and Father, to Him be glory and dominion forever.... REVELATION 1:5-6

Then Jesus said to His disciples, "If anyone desires to come after Me, let him deny himself, and take up his cross, and follow Me." MATTHEW 16:24

Physical Description

The brazen altar was located in the court near the gate. It was made of acacia wood overlaid with brass. Quite large, the brazen altar measured seven-and-one-half feet square with a height of four-and-one-half feet. Designed as an altar of burnt offerings, it was stout enough to support large pieces of animal carcass and was the proper height to facilitate the necessary firewood beneath the grate and the physical handling of the animal being sacrificed.

There were four horns upon the brazen altar. "*You shall make its horns on its four corners; its horns shall be of one piece with it. And you shall overlay it with* [brass]" (Exodus 27:2). The priest was to place some of the animal's blood on these four horns. The rituals involving sacrificial blood were imbued with sacred importance, especially when the priest took blood from the brazen altar into the Tabernacle. Here he placed the blood upon the four horns of the golden altar and sprinkled blood upon all vessels of the Tabernacle.

> *Moses ... took the blood of calves and goats, with water, scarlet wool, and hyssop, and sprinkled both* ***the book*** *itself and all* ***the people*** *... likewise he sprinkled with blood both* ***the tabernacle*** *and all* ***the vessels*** *of the ministry.* HEBREWS 9:19, 21, EMPHASIS ADDED

The influence of the blood was pervasive and profound. The life of the body is the blood. The sacrificial animal's life (blood) was sprinkled on everyone and everything having to do with the court and the Tabernacle. Without the shedding of this lifeblood and its proper application, there could be no remission of sin. The physical blood of Christ had to be shed according to the pattern that God established. The proper application of the Savior's blood on the lives of His people requires spiritual understanding. It is no longer literal blood that redeems. It is the life of the blood, or the Spirit of God's grace, which now pervades the entirety of our walk in Christ, the Anointed One.

The wood fire of the brazen altar was a daily reality. "*... it shall not be put out. And the priest shall burn wood on it every morning....*" (Leviticus 6:12). Smoke from the burning of the sacrificial animal on the brazen altar produced an aroma described as "*a sweet savour unto the LORD*" (Leviticus 6:21, KJV). The smoke with its aroma permeated the entire court. It represented the ever-present awareness among all believers that Christ died for their sin. Indeed, it is a sweet aroma—a heavenly atmosphere—wherein God's people are encouraged and uplifted by the influence of the Cross in their daily lives.

Spiritual Application

It is vital to recognize the Mosaic Tabernacle in the wilderness as a pattern of the true Temple treasures. Moses was given direct instruction from God to make the Tabernacle exactly according to the pattern shown to him. The Aaronic priesthood merely enacted a symbolic pattern of rites and rituals—and in particular, animal sacrifices—which signified pristine spiritual realities. An animal sacrificed unto God according to the exact prescription of Law was a sacred offering in the eyes of the Aaronic priesthood and the people of Israel. But they never perceived that their patterned rituals were only *shadows.* The shadows would be swallowed up by the glorious Light of Jesus Christ.

> *Their* [the Aaronic priesthood under Law] *work is connected with a mere earthly model of the real tabernacle in heaven; for when Moses was getting ready to build the tabernacle, God warned him to follow exactly the pattern of the heavenly tabernacle as shown to him on Mount Sinai.* HEBREWS 8:5, TLB

It is only in Christ, the Anointed One, that the earthly model reveals the secrets of the real, heavenly Temple treasures. In the analysis of the brazen altar it should be apparent that the requirement of animal sacrifice—and an offering of blood—was a pattern of the Savior's crucifixion. All who come to God will believe in the Son of God and that He died on the Cross for the sin of the world. "*...Behold! The Lamb of God who takes away the sin of the world!*" (John 1:29). It was the Father's plan—pattern—from the beginning of the ages that His only begotten Son would ultimately redeem mankind through the sacrifice of His physical life and blood upon the Cross. All who have embraced their redemption give honor and glory unto the Son because they recognize Him as "*...the Lamb slain from the foundation of the world*" (Revelation 13:8).

The Law Covenant, with its ritualistic sacrifice of animals, never delivered the people from a consciousness of sin. The weight of sin, the guilt of sin, the condemnation of sin—no sacred sacrificial rite under the Law could ever free the people from their human consciousness of a carnal nature. The force of the Law, and its exacting standards, made it obvious to every man and woman that they could never be justified through their own human efforts to fulfill the Law Covenant. Every animal sacrificed under the Law was a vivid reminder to the people of their bondage to carnality, corruption, and death.

The ministry of the Savior, His crucifixion on the Cross, and His Resurrection from the dead were anointed and exalted by the Father to inaugurate the New Covenant of grace and truth. The standard of righteousness under the Old Covenant of Law was not only fulfilled in Jesus Christ, but indeed His glorious gospel superceded the Law and triumphed over it.

> *He takes away the first* [Covenant of Law] *that He may establish the second* [Covenant of grace and truth]. *By that will* ***we have been sanctified through the offering of the body of Jesus Christ once for all.*** HEBREWS 10:9-10, EMPHASIS ADDED

The age of the Law Covenant was completed and the age of grace and truth began. In other words, two ages met together back to back. One age, of Law, was closed out and finished while the new age, of grace and truth, broke forth victoriously. "*...now* [two thousand years ago], *once at the end of the ages,* ***He has appeared to put away sin by the sacrifice of Himself***" (Hebrews 9:26, emphasis added). Upon the Savior's death hinged the course of the ages. The Law had served its purpose well. It proved to humanity that they could never be free through religious law and a natural Tabernacle with its literal priesthood, priestly vestments, vessels of sacred furniture, rites, rituals, and sacrifices. The Law wore humanity out and they wore it out.

> *In that He says, "A new covenant," He has made the first* [Law Covenant] *obsolete. Now what is becoming obsolete and growing old is ready to vanish away.* HEBREWS 8:13

The Old Testament Tabernacle with its code of Law was made obsolete when the Savior appeared as the living Temple of God. The living Temple replaced the dead pattern. The limitations and condemnation of the Law and its natural order of Temple sacrifices vanished away for all who gladly embraced the Son and His message of eternal salvation.

Great reverence is stirred within our hearts when we realize how carefully and patiently the Father established the Mosaic Tabernacle in ancient times—the pattern—so that we, His offspring, can comprehend the glory of the true Temple not made by hands. The Son, revealed as the Temple of God, overturned long centuries of spiritual darkness. On the Day of Pentecost the disciples knew by personal experience that they too were heirs of a Temple of indescribable power and glory.

Jesus died for sin one time. His singular death on the Cross established forgiveness of sin once and for all time. He will never die again. His crucifixion was a perfect work of redemption. Nothing done by any human can ever add or detract from the deliverance wrought by Christ's shed blood. Every aspect of His life, death, Resurrection, and ascension were precisely crafted by the Father from time immemorial. He alone was the sacrifice appointed by the Father before the ages began, whose singular martyrdom would atone for the separation between God and man.

The Tabernacle in the wilderness, with its ceaseless slaughter of animals, set the stage for many long centuries. Year after year, month after month, week after week, and day after day each animal sacrifice was enacted with meticulous detail according to the Law. The sacred blood was handled with honor. The Aaronic priesthood was dedicated to it. The people were in awe of it. Count up the dead carcasses, measure the amount of animal blood, and after centuries of sacrifice at the brazen altar, God's Spirit inspired the following startling assertion:

> ***Sacrifice and offering You did not desire; My ears You have opened. Burnt offering and sin offering You did not require.*** *Then I said, "Behold, I come; in the scroll of the book it is written of me. I delight to do Your will, O my God, and Your law is within my heart."* PSALM 40:6-8, EMPHASIS ADDED

The Spirit of God spoke words through the Old Testament prophets that were beyond the understanding of their time and place. Here, in the midst of centuries of the dedicated religious slaughter of animals, the Holy Spirit revealed a higher concept and order. The mystery of the pattern was to be revealed in the Son. His delight was to do the will of His Father; and the law of the Father's divine nature was written in the Son's heart. The concept of grace, after the Order of Melchizedek, was destined to replace the concept of Law, after the Order of Aaron.

Other prophets also wrote of a sacrifice more worthy than those animal sacrifices under the Law.

> *I desire mercy and not sacrifice, and the knowledge of God more than burnt offerings.* HOSEA 6:6

> *To do righteousness and justice is more acceptable to the LORD than* [animal] *sacrifice.* PROVERBS 21:3

One of the most critical blood sacrifices under the Law was accomplished at the time of Passover. The Passover celebrated the Israelites' deliverance from Egyptian bondage. Every Israelite family had been warned by God to slay a lamb and mark the door frames of their homes with the lamb's blood. In this way, the death angel would know to pass over the homes of the Israelites. Indeed, the death angel passed throughout Egypt at midnight to slay the firstborn of every Egyptian home—but the Israelite homes marked with the lamb's blood were spared.

It was this traumatic event that caused Pharaoh to send the Israelites out of Egypt.

God commanded the Israelites to reenact this sacrifice of the Passover lamb every year throughout their generations as a memorial to their deliverance from Egyptian bondage. Over fifteen hundred years later, they continued to kill the Passover lamb on the appointed evening. It was at this exact time when Jesus was crucified. (See Luke 22:1-15; John 18:28-39; and John 19:14.) While Jesus knew the symbolic meaning of the Passover, and understood that He was the Passover Lamb, yet the disciples did not recognize this truth until after His death and Resurrection.

> *For indeed* ***Christ, our Passover, was sacrificed for us.***
> 1 Corinthians 5:7, emphasis added

Here again we perceive God's handiwork in creating a type and shadow—a symbol—by which His people can gain vast spiritual insight. Depths of wisdom are revealed as the symbolic patterns are decoded by the Spirit. It seems the patterns were often quite complex, extensive, and required many religious works. The fulfillment of the pattern in Christ, however, is wonderfully direct and simple. The simplicity of Christ, the Anointed One, overcomes the complexity of Law. "*Christ gave himself to God for our sins as* ***one sacrifice for all time....*** *For by that* ***one offering*** *he made forever perfect in the sight of God all those whom he is making holy*" (Hebrews 10:12, 14, TLB, emphasis added).

Jesus endured the Cross because of the joy that was set before Him. He fully realized that the completeness of His inheritance as the Son of God awaited Him on the other side of the Cross. It was with this hope and assurance that He willingly accepted His responsibility to die for the sin of the world. His sacrifice for sin is now our possession as we embrace our inheritance in the Son.

We enter the gate of the court by faith and then approach the brazen altar with joy. No longer are we overwhelmed by the demands and requirements of the former Tabernacle. Instead of finding the never-ending accusation of guilt, we find God's all-embracing love and forgiveness. The Cross fulfilled the need of the brazen altar and freed us from any and all penalty.

The four horns of the brazen altar, located at its four upper corners, are spiritually significant. *Horns* is a term with several interesting definitions. In its most obvious sense, horns mean a projection; but it also means a flash, a cornet, rays of light, and power. The four horns, strong projections from the top of the brazen altar, point straight upward. Each horn makes a point. This type-and-shadow from the Old Testament is wonderfully revealed in the New Testament. Here the spiritual meaning of the four horns is clearly expressed:

> *But of him are ye in Christ Jesus, who of God is made unto us* ***wisdom****, and* ***righteousness****, and* ***sanctification****, and* ***redemption****.* 1 CORINTHIANS 1:30, KJV, EMPHASIS ADDED

The four physical horns point upward to Heaven—to heavenly places in Christ Jesus. His physical sacrifice upon the Cross pointed toward our spiritual inheritance in the Kingdom of Heaven. Indeed, He died for sin once to bring reconciliation with God, but in His Resurrection He is made unto us much more than the physical body hung on the Cross. Eternal concepts emerge from the brazen altar as the four horns: 1) wisdom, 2) righteousness, 3) sanctification, and 4) redemption.

The brazen altar, as a physical pattern, was fulfilled. The function and purpose of the physical Cross was also fulfilled in the Savior's death. Now the Cross is imbued with great spiritual power. It yields up the power of the Resurrection wherein we live and move in the realm of spiritual sacrifices. A great sense of victory and freedom emanate from this understanding of the brazen altar and its interrelationship with the Cross. We rejoice in spiritual sacrifices that are pleasing to the Father.

The Old Testament prophets wrote of these spiritual sacrifices:

> *I will offer to You* ***the sacrifice of thanksgiving,*** *and will call upon the name of the LORD.* PSALM 116:17, EMPHASIS ADDED

> ***I will sacrifice to You with the voice of thanksgiving;*** *I will pay what I have vowed.* ***Salvation is of the Lord.*** JONAH 2:9, EMPHASIS ADDED

The above verses testify of the grace found in the Son. The writers of the New Testament drew upon these Old Testament writings. It brought great consolation to the apostles when they realized the Holy Spirit had announced the grace of Christ in ancient times. *"Of this salvation the prophets have inquired and searched carefully, who prophesied of the grace that would come to you"* (1 Peter 1:10). Take note: they prophesied of the grace to be revealed in Christ. *"...the gospel of God which He promised before through His prophets in the Holy Scriptures"* (Romans 1:1-2).

Even though the prophets were confined to a Law-consciousness, God inspired them to write of the grace promised to future generations. Christ's crucifixion broke the confines of the Law Covenant. The meaning of His crucifixion and the power of His Resurrection fulfilled the Old Testament's prophetic writings. Our anointed Savior brought salvation, grace, and the Gospel of God. The confinement of the former Tabernacle's ritual and sacrifice is gone. Its bondage is broken. As living Temples of the living God, we now dwell in grace and offer spiritual sacrifices in the liberty of His Spirit.

> *Let my prayer be set before You* ***as incense****, the lifting up of my hands* ***as the evening sacrifice****.* PSALM 141:2, EMPHASIS ADDED

We no longer worship to satisfy the dictates of ritualistic law, but our prayers and uplifted hands are in response to His great infilling Spirit. The pages of the New Testament overflow with the love of the Father made known unto mankind through His Son. In the New Covenant of grace and truth we find this divine love, life, peace, joy, forgiveness, righteousness, and mercy. We receive these heavenly treasures as we willingly embrace God's will and let the divine principles of His Word have free course in our lives. "*... present your bodies a living sacrifice, holy, acceptable to God, which is your reasonable service*" (Romans 12:1). As vessels in the Lord's house, bought with a price, our lives are offered unto Him as living sacrifices.

> *You also, as living stones, are being built up* ***a spiritual house****, a holy priesthood, to offer up* ***spiritual sacrifices*** *acceptable to God through Jesus Christ.* 1 PETER 2:5, EMPHASIS ADDED

Spiritual sacrifices! They are acceptable to God through Christ. Joyous multitudes of believers gather together in the court—just inside the gate of faith—to celebrate the victory of the Cross. It is a spiritual realm, a dimension of grace, wherein the people offer up sacrifices of praise, honor, and thanksgiving for the deliverance they have found.

> *He* [Christ] *went into that greater, perfect tabernacle in heaven, not made by men nor part of this world, and once for all took blood into that inner room, the Holy of Holies, and sprinkled it on the mercy seat; but it was not the blood of goats and calves. No, he took his own blood, and with it he, by himself, made sure of our*

> *eternal salvation.... His sacrifice frees us from the worry of having to obey the old rules, and makes us want to serve the living God. For by the help of the eternal Holy Spirit, Christ willingly gave himself to God to die for our sins—he being perfect, without a single sin or fault.*
> Hebrews 9:11-14, TLB

These verses summarize the spiritual application of the brazen altar. The Aaronic priest entered the natural Tabernacle with sacrificial blood. Jesus, the High Priest of the Melchizedek Order, offered His own life as a spotless sacrifice unto God. Through the death of His body on the Cross, and the shedding of His own blood, the Son of God entered the Holy of Holies as the Forerunner and Captain of our eternal salvation. His sacrifice fulfilled the Law once and for all time. We are free from the curse of sin because of the Son.

Having entered the gate through faith in the Son, we have discovered the brazen altar and the great work of redemption that it represents. Redemption through the Cross is an accomplished fact. All we have to do is believe the good news. Faith in the Son and the work of the Cross causes the human soul to overflow with sincere praise. Our Elder Brother established an example of spiritual sacrifice unto God through the power of the Spirit. We—the heirs of salvation—offer spiritual sacrifices of praise, thanksgiving, and honor unto God.

> *Therefore by Him let us continually* ***offer the sacrifice of praise to God****, that is, the fruit of our lips, giving thanks to His name.* Hebrews 13:15, emphasis added

God offered His Son, a sacrifice for sin.
Forgiveness abounds; His new life I now win.

THE LAVER

Key Words: Examination and Cleansing

Significance

The laver signifies self-examination and cleansing through the effective use of God's Word. The New Testament refers to this purifying process as *sanctification.* Herein we judge and cleanse ourselves as we are washed in the water of the Word.

Supportive Scriptures

Examine me, O LORD, and prove [test] me; try my mind and my heart. PSALM 26:2

You were washed, you were sanctified, you were justified in the name of the Lord Jesus Christ and by the Spirit of our God. 1 CORINTHIANS 6:11, NIV

Christ loved the church and gave himself up for her to make her holy, cleansing her by the washing with water through the word. EPHESIANS 5:25-26, NIV

Let us draw near with a true heart in full assurance of faith, having our hearts sprinkled from an evil conscience and our bodies washed with pure water. HEBREWS 10:22

If we confess our sins, he is faithful and just, and will forgive our sins and cleanse us from all unrighteousness.
1 JOHN 1:9, RSV

Physical Description

The laver was a large brass bowl set on a brass pedestal. Lined with mirrors ("women's looking glasses") and filled with water, the laver was utilized by the priesthood to wash prior to performing priestly duties. It was located in the court between the brazen altar and the Tabernacle. "*Then the LORD spoke to Moses, saying: 'You shall also make a laver of* [brass], *with its base also of* [brass], *for washing. You shall put it between the tabernacle of meeting and the* [brazen] *altar. And you shall put water in it'*" (Exodus 30:17-18). The Bible provides little in the way of specific physical description or actual dimensions of the laver.

Spiritual Application

The laver, centrally located in the court, fulfilled a crucial role in the daily activities of the priesthood. The Aaronic priest had to conscientiously wash his hands and feet each day before putting on Aaron's garments. So vital was this act of examination and washing that the failure to properly fulfill the ordinance resulted in death. "*Aaron and his sons shall wash their hands and their feet in water from it* [the laver] *...lest they die*" (Exodus 30:19-20). This point is given such emphasis in the Bible that we must conclude that the laver's spiritual application to our lives is vital.

The laver reinforces the idea that there is a process, or preparation, which God honors among those who desire to enter their full inheritance. It is a spiritual obligation to wash hands and feet. The hands represent our ministry. We are all ministers as a royal priesthood in Christ. One must have clean hands in order to do the work of God: "*...which ... our hands* *have handled, of the Word of life"* (1 John 1:1, KJV). Unclean, or unrighteous, hands will always pollute the house of God.

The feet represent one's understanding. God's people are to be shod with the preparation of the gospel of peace. They are to walk in love. Jesus washed the feet of His disciples and stated that if their feet were clean it was enough; that is, if their understanding were pure then everything else would take care of itself. The fact that the Aaronic priest had to physically wash his hands and feet under the Old Covenant of Law is transcended in the New Covenant of grace and truth wherein we must clean up our lives according to the principles of God's Word.

The water in the laver was kept clean and pure. The brass bowl of the laver was lined with women's looking glasses, or mirrors. The priest would look into the pure water with its reflective mirrors as he washed himself. The water was symbolic of the Word of God. The women's looking glasses were symbolic of the New Testament writings. Each New Testament epistle was addressed to a particular church—an assembly of called-out people. Each assembly was perceived as a spiritual mother. A strong spiritual mother produced mature spiritual offspring. The mother consisted of a unified body of believers of all ages, backgrounds, dispositions, and degrees of spiritual maturity. This general corporate body was a spiritual woman who produced mature sons and daughters of God. The apostles wrote letters, or epistles, to these women, or assemblies. The women's looking glasses of the laver are representative of these New Testament epistles.

Today we interpret the laver as self-examination and cleansing. We examine our character in the reflective light of the New Testament epistles. Each epistle is like a woman's looking glass by which we can examine our shortcomings, weaknesses, character flaws, and personal temptations. We know we have salvation and forgiveness of sin because of our understanding of the brazen altar. Thus the laver's purpose is not to establish salvation and forgiveness. Instead, it urges us to look a little deeper into our character and provides the water of the Word for inner cleansing and renewal.

> ***Let a man examine himself****, and so let him eat of the bread* [truth] *and drink of the cup* [Spirit]. 1 CORINTHIANS 11:28, EMPHASIS ADDED

> ***Examine yourselves*** *as to whether you are in the faith. Test yourselves....* 2 CORINTHIANS 13:5, EMPHASIS ADDED

The strong presence of the laver shows that the priest, though he has entered the court, is in further need of cleansing. The positioning of the laver in the court clearly indicates there is an ongoing process of regeneration required of God's people. It is not enough to stay at the gate of faith or dwell continually at the brazen altar of spiritual sacrifices. Nor is it proper to push ahead toward the Tabernacle by our own self-will and human zeal. The laver draws one's attention to do some necessary self-examination and cleansing.

The Old Testament prophets were inspired by the Spirit to write of a spiritual dimension beyond the natural court, to a hope much greater than washing in literal water out of a brass basin.

> *Who can understand his errors? Cleanse me from secret faults.* PSALM 19:12

Secret faults and errors cannot be seen in a natural mirror nor washed away in natural water. The mirrors and water of the Mosaic Tabernacle never effectively changed the inner man. There was an obsessive concern with the natural man because their focus was on external, temporal, fleshly conditions. The inner man—subjected to the Law of a temporal Tabernacle—went unexamined and unwashed.

Conversely, the light of truth provided in the New Testament writings reveals our errors, and the pure water of the Word cleanses us from secret faults. The cleansing value of God's Word reaches the inner recesses of the human soul. It is so very important that God's people reflect on His Word in order to receive the Word's reflective power. With meditative reflection, we can partake of the sanctifying virtue of God's Word.

> *Who may ascend into the hill* [high places] *of the LORD? Or who may stand in His holy place* [the Temple]*? He who has clean hands and a pure heart....* PSALM 24:3-4

Only the Word of God can make our hands clean in the sight of God and bring purity of heart. Personal transformation of one's character is essential.

> *Wash yourselves, make yourselves clean....* ISAIAH 1:16

We are admonished to fully utilize the laver. The admonition is given so that we might maintain a balanced perspective of the court and the Temple. The laver, along with every other vessel in the court, is not to be despised. Every vessel and all aspects of the court are holy unto the Lord. We need to always remember that each vessel of the court is ordained of God. He instructed Moses to anoint all vessels of both the court and the Holy Places to signal their essential purpose in God.

None of the vessels of the Lord's house, including the laver, are found out in the tents. Our faith in the Son of God separates us from the carnal masses that dwell outside the court in the tents of the ungodly. Through faith in the Savior we are members of God's household. There is only one entrance into this wondrous household: faith in the Son of God. He is the door, and all who attempt to claim the Temple treasures any other way are found to be thieves and robbers.

Be clean, you who bear the vessels of the LORD. ISAIAH 52:11

Those of noble heart, who aspire to the goodness of God, gladly embrace the opportunity provided by the laver to cleanse themselves. Each man and woman should seriously consider that their awesome inheritance in the Temple involves bearing the vessels of the Lord. We—the people of God—are to bear the holy vessels of the Temple so that the world around us might be blessed, and ultimately, transformed. The laver is an opportunity to take personal responsibility. It purifies our motives. Complacency and self-satisfaction are replaced by discipline and inspiration. The laver establishes a serious-minded commitment in our hearts to God and to His people.

Wash me, and I shall be whiter than snow.... Create in me a clean heart, O God, and renew a steadfast spirit within me. PSALM 51:7, 10

The cry of every earnest heart—*Wash me, O God*—finds the looking glasses and pure water of the laver a pleasant consolation. Here we can wash away the grit and grime of carnality. We can use the laver to renew our original commitment to God. Every soul, when first saved at the gate of faith, experiences the wonderful awareness of a clean heart. The newborn soul cries a joyful "Yes!" to the "Amazing grace ... that saved a wretch like me." Then the cares and burdens of life go to work to cloud that original wonder of salvation. The laver addresses these challenges of daily life by washing away the imperfections and contaminations of a carnal world. The laver continually renews and purifies. Many believers have never yet been taught the benefits of examination and cleansing which are available in the laver.

A process of cleansing was accomplished through the Word spoken by the Savior to His disciples. The Word by which He washed His disciples would later be written within the pages of the New Testament. Always the teacher, Jesus continually taught the Word of truth to His disciples.

> *You are already clean because of the word which I have spoken to you.* JOHN 15:3

The Word of truth imparts great cleansing virtue in the realm, or dimension, of the laver. Therefore the Lord demonstrated the importance of the laver in His own ministry.

The Aaronic priesthood of the Old Testament was called to daily obligations in both the court and the Tabernacle. Washing in the laver was always a prerequisite. They examined and washed themselves in the laver as a point of Law. If we understand the laver as a symbol of spiritual realities, then we will heed the example to cleanse ourselves regularly in the water of the Word. The key point of difference is that we wash the inner man by grace through the help of the Holy Spirit, rather than the outer [flesh] man according to religious ritual.

The goal of those in the court is to enter the Holy Places of the Temple. Ordinary common sense would tell a person to get cleaned up before approaching the king. Our King has promised an inheritance of most precious treasure, and we will be prepared to receive it when we approach Him properly.

> *Therefore, having these promises, beloved,* ***let us cleanse ourselves from all filthiness of the flesh and spirit,*** *perfecting holiness in the fear of God.* 2 CORINTHIANS 7:1, EMPHASIS ADDED

Consider that these words were written to a committed and anointed people, as were all the New Testament epistles. And yet the Apostle Paul urges them to seek out this cleansing process. He refers to the ongoing process of *perfecting holiness*. The perfecting of holiness in the fear of God just means that we approach Him with profound reverence and respect. We remember the cloud of glory and pillar of fire, which abode upon the Tabernacle in the wilderness. We have been given better promises as the heirs of salvation, which surpass the glory of the former Tabernacle. These promises instill humility and a desire to walk in ways well-pleasing to Him.

> *If we confess our sins, He is faithful and just to forgive us our sins and to* ***cleanse us from all unrighteousness.***
> 1 JOHN 1:9, EMPHASIS ADDED

Every born-again child of God must cope with this inner conflict. The Cross established complete forgiveness of sin, and yet human nature is ever-present to steal away the victory. The above Scripture makes it quite plain that God's people must deal with sin and unrighteousness. We are called of God through Christ to grow up and gain maturity in our mind, in our heart, and in our character. It is a process of regeneration through the Spirit and Word. Sin means to miss the mark. The mark is Jesus Christ, the Anointed Savior, our Elder Brother and Captain of Salvation who has already made the way and provided all that we need to be transformed into His image and likeness. We press toward the mark of the prize of the high calling of God in Christ.

The court and the Tabernacle were given by God as a pattern of our spiritual journey. If there were no journey, no regeneration, no processing, no progression, no transformation, then God would have had Moses build the Ark of the Covenant and nothing more. Believe in the Lord—and presto!—instantly we are in the Ark to stay. But as a true Father, He was wise. God knew from the beginning that instant gratification does not produce great character.

The Father's objective is to produce mature, fully developed sons and daughters. And He wants us to realize that the pattern shown to Moses involves the magnificent purpose of His will for each of His children. The pattern is multifaceted. It provides a number of unique vessels assigned to represent marvelous realms of spiritual progression into the greatness of God. Everyone who enters the gate receives this vast provision of opportunity to attain to God's highest.

> *Not by works of righteousness which we have done, **but according to His mercy He saved us, through the washing of regeneration and renewing of the Holy Spirit.*** TITUS 3:5, EMPHASIS ADDED

The washing of regeneration indicates continual spiritual progression. We are called to grow up into the fullness of the Son. If we level off or falter, God in His mercy will help us along our way in this magnificent obsession to partake of His divine nature and the glory of His Kingdom. The renewing of the Holy Spirit also emphasizes the vibrant transformational power that God invests in His children. We are not limited to an once-in-a-lifetime experience with God's Spirit. Our Father is the merciful source of spiritual renewal.

The Father loves us as His own children. His provisions for us are exceedingly abundant. Good natural parents want their children to have an abundance of opportunities for advancement. Parents realize that trial and error, along with success and failure, are a normal part of their children's development. In spite of their children's shortcomings, misguided endeavors, and even outright failures, good parents will offer continued love and encouragement, always with the hope that new opportunities will allow their children to grow and prosper. In like manner, our heavenly Father provides not only challenges and corrections, but also bountiful opportunities for growth and prosperity.

God's grace kindles remarkable concepts such as *re*birth, *re*conciliation, *re*newal, *re*generation, and *re*demption. The presence of the laver in the court is comforting. Its reflective surface brimming with pure water of the Word is always available for examination and cleansing.

I examine myself and wash in the laver,
I commit my life to the Word of the Savior.

AARON'S GARMENTS

Key Words: The Lord, Our Righteousness

Significance

Aaron's garments signify total spiritual dedication and singleness of mind unto the Lord. God's righteous covering takes precedence in the believer's life. Recognition of the Lord as our righteousness prepares us to enter the Temple.

Supportive Scriptures

The light of the body is the eye: if therefore thine eye be single, thy whole body shall be full of light. MATTHEW 6:22, KJV

I will greatly rejoice in the LORD, my soul shall be joyful in my God; for He has clothed me with the garments of salvation, He has covered me with the robe of righteousness.... ISAIAH 61:10

He put on righteousness as a breastplate, and a helmet of salvation on His head.... ISAIAH 59:17

One thing I have desired of the LORD, that will I seek: that I may dwell in the house of the LORD all the days of my life, to behold the beauty of the LORD, and to inquire in His temple. PSALM 27:4

All the promises of God in Him are Yes, and in Him Amen, to the glory of God through us. 2 CORINTHIANS 1:20

I press toward the goal for the prize of the upward call of God in Christ Jesus. PHILIPPIANS 3:14

Physical Description

Aaron's garments were a requirement of priesthood. No garment; no priesthood. We should note that the priest put on the garments only after washing in the laver.

*You shall make holy garments for Aaron … **for glory and for beauty**…. These are the garments which they shall make: a breastplate, an ephod, a robe, a skillfully woven tunic, a turban, and a sash. So they shall make holy garments for Aaron your bother and his sons, that he may minister to Me as priest.* EXODUS 28:2, 4, EMPHASIS ADDED

The garments were made of linen royally colored with blue, purple, and scarlet. (See Leviticus 16:4; Exodus 39:1.) Moses, in obedience to God, consecrated both the priesthood and their garments with oil and blood. (See Leviticus 8:30.) The oil typifies the anointing of the Spirit, and the blood typifies the Savior's sacrificial death on the Cross. Aaron's garments are hereby given strong symbolic emphasis.

Spiritual Application

We approach the veil of the Holy Place with great focus and singleness of purpose. We are clothed in spiritual garments by which we are prepared to enter the Tabernacle not made by hands. Our progression through the court has sharpened our spiritual senses, focused our minds, and filled us with an attitude of thankfulness and joy in the Lord. His grace has lifted our souls, and He has given us *"the garment of praise for the spirit of heaviness..."* (Isaiah 61:3).

> *Let Your priests be* ***clothed with righteousness,*** *and let Your saints shout for joy.... I will also* ***clothe her priests with salvation,*** *and her saints shall shout aloud for joy.*
> PSALM 132:9, 16, EMPHASIS ADDED

The human soul experiences joy in the presence of the Lord's own righteousness and salvation. It is truly a joyous realization that we do not have to stand alone in this life as a naked human soul, but we can be clothed with eternal garments. The weight of human life is referred to as *the spirit of heaviness.* It consists of life's worries, cares, fears, burdens, defeats, and despair. Gladly, we exchange the spirit of heaviness for garments of praise. We lay aside our old negative human attitudes. We relinquish the carnal covering of the human spirit in exchange for the righteousness and salvation of the Holy Spirit. The Temple of God is holy and we must be properly clothed in the righteous covering of the Lord's presence in order to enter the first veil of the Temple.

Consider carefully the fact that Moses anointed the priestly garments with oil and blood. As stated earlier, the anointing of oil refers to the presence of the Holy Spirit; the anointing of blood refers to the redeeming power of the Cross. It is this anointing of abundant Spirit and grace which exerts its leadership over those who submit their human will to the will of God. The anointing of the Spirit is not random, but it imparts a strong sense of purpose and destination. The unction of the Spirit will always lead and direct the seeker into greater truth and illumination. To be more specific, the Spirit of God earnestly desires that we enter the fullness of our Temple treasures.

The Holy Spirit is the Comforter gently leading us into heavenly places. We do not walk alone into the Temple of

God. His Spirit dwells within and upon our lives. It is by His spiritual presence and covering, and not by our own might or power. Our entrance through the first veil of the Holy Place requires a prayerful attitude combined with sharp mental focus. It is only as we abide within the covering of the Spirit that we can lay aside every human burden and distraction. A double-minded condition is unstable and will only hinder our entrance into the Holy Place. We are encouraged by the Spirit to have a girded-up mind and a single eye. It is the Spirit that creates the inner singleness of mind such that all of our earthly distractions fade away.

> *Therefore* ***gird up the loins of your mind****, be sober, and rest your hope fully upon the grace that is to be brought to you at the revelation of Jesus Christ.* 1 PETER 1:13, EMPHASIS ADDED

This reference to *loins of your mind* shows that the apostles understood the symbolic nature of Aaron's garments. The old Aaronic priesthood wore linen breeches and robes to cover their physical loins. But the new man of the Spirit is informed that the loins of his mind matter most of all. *Gird up* means to get focused. It is interesting to note that the physical human brain has both a right and a left hemisphere. These two hemispheres are referred to as loins. The number two represents the Two Witnesses of the Father and Son. We have spiritual loins of the mind that hold the precious seed-Word of God's truth. To gird up the loins of the mind means to get totally focused on the Word of God. Give His truth the preeminent place in our mind.

We are to rest our hope fully—completely—upon the grace that is to be given at the revelation of Jesus Christ. This again emphasizes the idea of girding up the mind, singling the inner eye, and getting properly focused. We are to *rest* [our] *hope* upon a further unfolding of God's grace as we proceed into the Temple. There is always hopefulness in the Spirit. There is hope to enter into a greater measure of grace which becomes ours when the indwelling Christ is revealed.

We can apply this phrase—*the revelation of Jesus Christ*—to our personal advancement through the court, the Holy Place, and the Holy of Holies. There is indeed a revelation of the Son of God in the court. Yet a more powerful expression of the Son awaits us in the Holy Places of the spiritual Temple. The Son of God is revealed as light which increasingly shines from the east unto the west: that is, from the eastern gate of the court unto the golden Ark of the Holy of Holies. The Apostle Peter is not telling us to get ready to go to Heaven someday to meet the Lord, nor is he saying to wait for the future coming of the Lord. Instead, he urges the people of God to prepare to enter into the Temple. There, in the deep presence of spiritual Holy Places, God's people receive revelation of the Son, which they never experienced in the court.

We must prepare ourselves to experience a greater revelation, a more dynamic manifestation, of the Lord. The Word of God gives us awesome hope *and* tells us how to bring the hope into reality. Gird up the mind. Be serious about moving on in God. Have hope for a greater expression of the Lord's inexhaustible wisdom and life. This is the attitude of expectation that leads to a greater measure of the knowledge of the Son. It is the spiritual condition of Aaron's garments.

The Son of God instructs His people, as follows:

> *Let your loins be girded about, and your lights burning.*
> LUKE 12:35, KJV

Again a proper spiritual attitude is emphasized. One must be ready and prepared to meet the Lord in a deeper context. He is saying to be prepared to receive further understanding of the Word. Be alert to the leading of the Spirit. A natural man, preparing to receive an important guest, gets properly dressed and lights the lamps in his house. We must do this spiritually if we hope to receive a greater visitation of the Son of God.

The Apostle Paul drew upon the symbolic value of Aaron's garments in Ephesians 6:13-17, wherein he also added the idea of spiritual armor. Paul enumerates the tremendous attributes of a spiritual covering. He encourages the people of God to take the whole armor of God, having:

- Loins girt with truth
- The breastplate of righteousness
- Feet shod with the gospel of peace
- The shield of faith
- The helmet of salvation
- The sword of the Spirit, which is the Word of God

This describes a spiritual condition similar to Aaron's garments. It is the unseen condition of the inner man just as God sees him in the Spirit. The soul is covered with the attributes of salvation, energized by the Holy Spirit, and strengthened by God's own power.

In another epistle Paul makes the same vital point in an abbreviated form: "*Let us who are of the day be sober, putting on the breastplate of faith and love, and as a helmet the hope of salvation*" (1 Thessalonians 5:8). We may never wear a natural breastplate or helmet. But we will grow in character to embrace faith, love, and salvation. In our walk with God, we will learn the virtue of praise, and we will appreciate that we are clothed with the Lord our righteousness. The outer components of Aaron's garments are emblematic of our inner spiritual development.

Twice in the New Testament the Apostle Paul refers to the breastplate. These references to the breastplate, combined with the detailed description provided in the Book of Exodus (see Exodus 28:4-30; 39:8-21), make it a very important part of Aaron's garments. The breastplate covered the heart. It consisted of the ephod—a type of shoulder harness—that was made of linen cloth intricately woven of gold, blue, purple, and scarlet thread. Two onyx stones, each engraved with the names of six tribes of Israel, were fastened in gold settings upon the two shoulders of the ephod.

The ephod supported the breastplate. Its linen cloth, designed with the same intricate beauty as the ephod, was folded into a square and connected to the ephod with braided gold chains. Twelve precious stones were fastened to the breastplate: four rows of three stones each. And each of the twelve stones was engraved with the name of a tribe of Israel.

> *Aaron shall bear the names of the sons of Israel on the breastplate of judgment over his heart, when he goes into the holy place, as a memorial before the* LORD *continually.* EXODUS 28:29

The number twelve often indicates governmental perfection, or complete divine governance. We can conclude that the breastplate of twelve stones symbolizes the complete family of God—a spiritual Israel of all who have been born from above. The breastplate covers our heart with divinely appointed responsibility. We enter the Holy Places of the Temple as representatives of God's people. The Temple is not designed for self-seeking or self-gratification. We are ambassadors of Christ, we carry a spiritual burden for His people, and He has anointed us as a royal priesthood to bring forth Temple treasures that bless His people.

The twelve names engraved upon the onyx stones were also engraved upon the stones of the breastplate. Surely this portrays a spiritual burden upon both the shoulders and the heart—a sincere care and love for humanity. Consider that the number twelve points to the ultimate good news destined for all nations of mankind.

Paul referred to the *breastplate of righteousness*, and also the *breastplate of faith and love.* These spiritual virtues cover the heart; that is, the old human motives are overcome by the precious stones of divine character. Spiritual integrity prevails. The Lord's righteousness becomes our heartbeat. Faithfulness to God and His people, motivated by divine love, are the heart of the matter in the Temple.

Two components of somewhat mystical nature were added to the breastplate. *"You shall put in the breastplate of judgment the Urim and the Thummin, and they shall be over Aaron's heart when he goes in* [the Holy of Holies] *before the LORD"* (Exodus 28:30). The meaning of these terms, Urim and Thummin, are significant: *lights and perfections*. The Bible gives very little information concerning the Urim and Thummin. Since the breastplate consisted of twelve stones, it is a reasonable assumption that Urim and Thummin were also precious stones. Their meaning—lights and perfections—would indicate stones of exquisite beauty when illumined by light.

Urim and Thummin were used as a means of communication between God and man. The priest would enter the Holy of Holies to rest on the Mercy Seat in the presence of God's *shekinah* glory. The Urim, illumined by the *shekinah*, shone its brilliance through the translucence of the Thummin to light up the twelve stones. When the *shekinah* glory illumined the breastplate in this manner, the answer to the priest's query was in the affirmative as a decisive "Yes," or a positive "Go." When the question was tribal in nature, the *shekinah* glory would illumine a particular stone, or stones, in the breastplate, for as we have seen each of the twelve stones was labeled by tribal name. By the lighting of a stone, or stones, serious tribal questions were resolved.

When we apply the symbolic significance of the breastplate to the New Testament, it takes on broader ramifications. The illumination of the breastplate typified spiritual hierarchy. Father (Urim) illumined the Son (Thummin) who in turn illumined the twelve apostles (twelve stones). Through this hierarchal method, the Word of God went forth to all the people (the tribes, or nations).

The analysis of the breastplate highlights the importance of Aaron's garments. It symbolizes the crucial need for the divine covering of God. We need to be clothed upon by His mighty anointing. This kind of terminology—related to spiritual covering and clothing—is used extensively in the Book of Revelation. Its emphasis on white linen robes indicates that one is becoming a partaker of the divine nature. Consider the spiritual implications of the white linen garments while carefully reading these verses:

> *He who overcomes shall be* ***clothed in white garments....*** REVELATION 3:5, EMPHASIS ADDED

> *I counsel you to buy from Me ...* ***white garments****, that you may be clothed, that the shame of your nakedness may not be revealed....* REVELATION 3:18, EMPHASIS ADDED

> *Then a* ***white robe*** *was given to each of them....* REVELATION 6:11, EMPHASIS ADDED

> *...a great multitude which no one could number, of all nations, tribes, peoples, and tongues, standing before the throne and before the Lamb,* ***clothed with white robes*** *... saying, "Salvation belongs to our God who sits on the throne, and to the Lamb!"* REVELATION 7:9-10, EMPHASIS ADDED

> *These are the ones who come out of the great tribulation, and* ***washed their robes and made them white in the blood of the Lamb****.* REVELATION 7:14, EMPHASIS ADDED

And to her was granted that she should be arrayed in fine linen, clean and white: for ***the fine linen is the righteousness of saints.*** REVELATION 19:8, KJV, EMPHASIS ADDED

The above six passages emphasize our need to be clothed spiritually. The final verse concisely defines the fine white linen garment: *the fine linen is the righteousness of saints.* The fact that we require the righteous covering of the Lord highlights our previous condition as unregenerate, carnal humans. Throughout the Scriptures it is made evident that there are both carnal coverings and spiritual coverings. A carnal covering results from human trust in human ways. Trust in any form of human power or wisdom is vanity when compared to the covering of God's Spirit. Trust in an earthly covering is nothing more than fig leaves in God's sight—it is the same as being spiritually naked.

Under penalty of death the Aaronic priest entered the Tabernacle without his priestly garments. Today we take this symbolic lesson to heart. We are taught of the Lord to clothe ourselves in His spiritual garments. A white robe, representative of God's own righteousness, is the inheritance of God's people. It is indeed a wonderful inheritance in which we cover our nakedness of the soul with His robe of righteousness, His garment of praise, His spiritual armor, and in every manner to be covered by His Holy Spirit.

We approach the Holy Place of the Temple with keen spiritual focus. Our experience in the court has prepared us to enter the Temple. The importance of the court is not to be minimized, for the court provides the essential transformation out of darkness into light. It plants us in the faith of the Son of God. It establishes the new inner birth into the Kingdom of God. However, it was not the intention of the Son, or the apostles, that God's people would settle down in the court forever. They taught growth, progress, and advancement into the Temple.

If then you were raised with Christ, ***seek*** *those things which are above, where Christ is, sitting at the right hand of God.* ***Set your mind on things above, not on things on the earth.*** *For you died, and your life is hidden with Christ in God.* ***When Christ who is our life appears, then you also will appear with Him in glory.*** COLOSSIANS 3:1-4, EMPHASIS ADDED

The glory of Christ appears in the Temple. The Scriptures state plainly that Christ is our life, that He dwells in us by the Spirit, and that we are the Temple of God. These are spiritual ideas, spiritual insights from on high, and they help lift us into the spiritual heights of heavenly places in Christ—that is, in the anointing of the Spirit. We are to seek these heavenly realms that are above. We are to set our mind on the Holy Spirit, fully realizing that we are born again into the new life of the Anointed One.

God is Spirit, and those who worship Him must worship in spirit and truth. JOHN 4:24

The Spirit of the Lord is stirring the hearts of His people to enter the Temple. With great vigor the Spirit urges us: Ask. Seek. Knock. Get spiritually focused and prepare to enter the Temple of the living God. *"Ask, and it will be given to you; seek, and you will find; knock, and it will be opened to you"* (Matthew 7:7). God will not withhold any good thing from those who walk uprightly. But He does expect His people to seek Him with all their heart, mind, and strength.

I love those who love me, and those who seek me diligently will find me. PROVERBS 8:17

Let the hearts of those rejoice who seek the LORD*! Seek the* LORD *and His strength; seek His face evermore!"*
PSALM 105:3-4

The call of the Almighty is upon His people to move forward into the glorious depths of His Temple.

MY MIND IS SINGLED; MY HEART HUMBLY OBEYS.
MY SOUL IS CLOTHED WITH GARMENTS OF PRAISE.

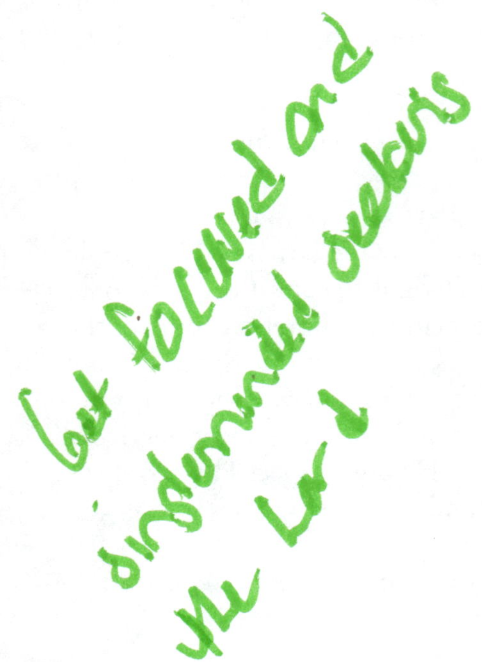

PART TWO

The Holy Place

There is a river whose streams shall make glad
the city of God, the holy place of the
tabernacle of the Most High.
God is in the midst of her, she shall not be moved;
God shall help her, just at the break of dawn.
Psalm 46:4-5

For Christ has entered into heaven itself,
to appear now before God as our Friend.
It was not in the earthly place of worship
that He did this, for that was merely a copy of
the real temple in heaven.
Hebrews 9:24, TLB

FIRST VEIL

Key Words: Divine Government

Significance

The first veil with its five golden pillars signifies divine government. It is the government established upon the apostles and the prophets with Jesus Christ as the Chief Cornerstone. Religious self-consciousness and self-will drop off dramatically at the first veil. A greater presence of the Lord exerts its dominion.

Supportive Scriptures

"Most assuredly, I say to you, he who receives whomever I send receives Me; and he who receives Me receives Him who sent Me." JOHN 13:20

"I [Christ] *have chosen you, and ordained you, that ye should go and bring forth fruit...."* JOHN 15:16, KJV

Speak these things, exhort, and rebuke with all authority. Let no one despise you.... TITUS 2:15

"And he who overcomes, and keeps My works until the end, to him I will give power over the nations ... as I also have received from My Father." REVELATION 2:26-27

"He who overcomes, I will make him a pillar in the temple of My God, and he shall go out no more...."
REVELATION 3:12

Physical Description

The entrance into the Tabernacle faced eastward in direct alignment with the gate of the court. There was a natural progression from the gate to the brazen altar to the laver to Aaron's garments to the veil of the Holy Place.

The veil, supported by five golden pillars, hung nearly to the ground so that the priest had to humbly bow to enter the Holy Place. The linen veil, beautifully designed *"of blue, and purple, and scarlet, and fine twined linen, of needlework"* (Exodus 36:37, KJV) was overlaid with animal skins, as we shall see.

Recall that the Tabernacle was composed of both the Holy Place and the Holy of Holies. The wall of the Tabernacle was built of vertical boards overlaid with gold. These gold-covered boards lined the two sides of the Tabernacle, as well as the back end. This board framework was covered by a tent composed of four types of material. White linen, embossed with cherubim, was the inner covering. This was followed by a second covering of goat hair, which was followed by a third covering of rams' skins dyed red, and this received a fourth covering of badger skins. Thus the interior of the Tabernacle was lovely. Its two sidewalls and the back wall were lined with the vertical, gold-covered boards. The ceiling was fine linen cloth delicately patterned of blue, purple, and scarlet with embroidered cherubim. The two veils, one for the Holy Place and one for the Holiest, were also of the same fine linen with its royal colors. The veil of the Holiest was sewn with cherubim whereas the Holy Place veil lacked these celestial winged figures.

In contrast to the lovely interior, however, the exterior of the tabernacle was rough and unattractive with its outer layer of badger skins. As mentioned, even the entrance to the Tabernacle was covered by the rough hides of animals.

Spiritual Application

This striking contrast between the lovely interior of the Temple versus the rough exterior is representative of God's people. We have an inner man of the Spirit who is clothed with the righteousness of God's golden inheritance. But we also have an outer fleshly man who performs ordinary human tasks and must function within the confines of human society. Though the outer man perishes, yet the inner man is renewed day-by-day. The Savior pointed to this dichotomy in these words: *"In the world you will have tribulation; but be of good cheer, I have overcome the world"* (John 16:33). And again He said, *"...the kingdom of God is within you"* (Luke 17:21).

The Temple treasures dwell deep within the soul. They are not readily apparent to the casual onlooker. Those who looked upon the Mosaic Tabernacle from its exterior saw nothing but rough animal skins. But those priests who were privileged to enter the Tabernacle saw exquisite golden beauty. God was wise to provide us with this contrast so that we would understand an important truth concerning His people. Do not judge by the seeing of the natural eye. Do not judge the souls of His people by their rough outer visage—indeed, it was spoken of our Savior that *"...His visage was marred more than any man"* (Isaiah 52:14).

> *He has no form or comeliness; and when we see Him, there is no beauty that we should desire Him.... And we hid, as it were, our faces from Him; He was despised, and we did not esteem Him.* ISAIAH 53:2-3

Those who rejected and persecuted the Son of God judged Him according to the flesh. They looked upon Him with natural eyes only. They could only perceive the Son of Man, but not the Son of God.

We must overlook the rough badger skins—the rough-hewn exterior—of God's people in order to discover the treasures that dwell within. It was God's wisdom to hide the treasures of His Kingdom in common and humble human vessels. *"We have this treasure in earthen vessels, that the excellence of the power may be of God and not of us"* (2 Corinthians 4:7).

We go beyond the court-consciousness by approaching, and entering, the first veil that leads into the Holy Place. The first veil with its five golden pillars separates the court from the Holy Place. The people of God who dwell only in the court are separated from the inner treasures of the Holy Place by this spiritual veil. As an analogy, the unbelievers who dwell out in the tents are separated from the treasures of the court by the gate of faith. These veils provide entrance into the court and the Temple respectively. On the other hand, these veils also provide separation. The veils, although of intangible substance, are imbued with the force of divine government. There is an administration of faith in the Son of God that governs the gate of the court. In a similar manner, there is an administration of divine government—wrought through the authority of the Son—which holds dominion at the first veil of the Holy Place.

Spiritual order prevails throughout the court, the Holy Place, and the Holy of Holies. God is not the author of confusion. He is order personified in the Temple not made by hands. *"Let all things be done decently and in order"* (1 Corinthians 14:40). It is important to realize it was God who established the order that governs the Temple. He established this order on the divine principles of His immutable Word. We are instructed to do all things decently according to His order. He has established principles of governance that He highly honors and blesses. To enter the Holy Place we willingly, and gladly, acknowledge the veil with its five pillars.

When the Aaronic priest humbly lowered himself to crawl beneath the first veil, he was making a symbolic gesture of honor unto the government of God. This same attitude of honor and reverence resonates in the heart of each seeker who desires to enter the Holy Place today. One does not enter the Holy Place through self-will. Rather, one who offers a humble attitude is invited by the Spirit to enter in. *"The fear of the LORD is the instruction of wisdom, and before honor is humility"* (Proverbs 15:33).

Humility marks the path of all who enter the deep places in God. The pride and conceit of earthly religion hold no merit in spiritual matters. One who seeks the honor of men will often find it in the court, but never in the Holy Place. Jesus taught the principle of humility:

> *"Whoever humbles himself as this little child is the greatest in the kingdom of heaven."* MATTHEW 18:4

> *"Whoever exalts himself will be humbled, and he who humbles himself will be exalted."* MATTHEW 23:12

We humble ourselves willingly, gladly, and joyfully unto the first veil, the government of God, because we truly honor His authority and power in our lives. This has nothing to do with a show of humility in the eyes of men. It is not a self-willed act motivated by covetousness to usurp the royal treasures. This humility is genuine, a fruit of the Holy Spirit, and the result of God's grace in our lives.

> *He gives more grace. Therefore He says: "God resists the proud, but gives grace to the humble."...humble yourselves in the sight of the Lord, and He will lift you up.* JAMES 4:6,10

It is very encouraging when we recognize the divine nature of our God as revealed in His Son—that He is gracious, longsuffering, and kind. He gives grace to the humble. He looks on the sincere heart with mercy. He has readied an inheritance for His people in the Temple from the foundation of the world. We can cast all our care upon Him and He will ever be the faithful steward of our souls. We can seek His best and most beauteous treasures and He will freely give more than we can ask or think. Yet it pleases God that we understand and honor His order. His heavenly government radiates the light of His glory and immortality, and it is with humility and reverence that we enter His presence.

> *The sacrifices of God are a broken spirit, a broken and a contrite heart—these, O God, You will not despise.*
> PSALM 51:17

The Savior embodied the government of God and spoke with divine authority. Yet He never manifested earthly pride or human conceit. The Son always acknowledged the Father. This open acknowledgment of the Father's authority highlighted the Son's ministry. Jesus willingly and joyfully submitted to the Father's will, and this righteous attitude pleased the Father.

The apostles were empowered by the Father and Son with great authority, and yet the same humble quality of character highlighted their ministries. Great authority and great humility are generally mutually exclusive in human government. In the eyes of arrogant self-made leaders, humility is looked upon as weakness. The Son and the apostles turned the world upside down by introducing a kingdom that is above carnal perception. In the divine government of God's Kingdom, humility is a prerequisite of authority.

Notice in the following verses the authority available in God's Kingdom as it was demonstrated in the Son:

> *When Jesus had ended these sayings, that the people were astonished at His teaching, for* ***He taught them as one having authority****, and not as the scribes.* MATTHEW 7:28-29, EMPHASIS ADDED

> *"...What a word this is! For* ***with authority and power He commands*** *the unclean spirits, and they come out."* LUKE 4:36, EMPHASIS ADDED

The Son imparted His authority to His disciples. We do well to honor these divinely chosen vessels who walked with humility among the human family—even unto persecution, public beatings, and eventual martyrdom.

> *He called His twelve disciples together and* ***gave them power and authority*** *over all demons, and to cure diseases.* LUKE 9:1, EMPHASIS ADDED

This power and authority emanates from the Temple. Contemporary Christianity knows little of divine government. Christian leadership—ministers, preachers, pastors, and priests—usually dwell in the court. Therefore the people, as a general rule, are never taught their inheritance of Temple treasures. There is no voice of instruction concerning spiritual order as it relates to the court and the Temple. Few and far between are the vessels of anointed authority to lead the people through the first veil.

The people of the virgin Church knew the secrets of true worship within the first veil. Indeed, the author and founder of their faith had walked among men as a living demonstration of the Temple. His immediate disciples and apostles were transformed into the image of the pattern-Son, so that they also entered the fullness of their Temple inheritance. The voice of divine government spoke through the Savior. The same voice spoke through the apostles. Whenever the voice of divine government spoke, the first veil of the Temple was opened in the lives of the people.

The way into the Temple remained open as long as the voice of divine authority continued speaking. The Apostle Peter, a pillar in the Temple, influenced multitudes to enter the Temple. He well understood the function and purpose of the court, but he always taught the people to grow in grace and knowledge—that is, to embrace the full potential inherent in the Word of God. Peter taught others the secrets he had learned from his Lord and Savior.

> *Yes, all of you be submissive to one another, and be clothed with humility, for "God resists the proud, but gives* ***grace to the humble." Therefore humble yourselves under the mighty hand of God, that He may exalt you in due time.*** 1 PETER 5:5-6, EMPHASIS ADDED

Take careful note of Peter's reference to the hand of God. The hand of God is His anointed governmental ministry. His hand is a five-fold ministry which the Apostle Paul enumerates in Ephesians 4:11-13, as follows:

- Apostles
- Prophets
- Evangelists
- Pastors
- Teachers

What is the purpose of the hand, or ministry, of God? Paul explains in the same passage: it is "*...for the equipping of the saints for the work of ministry, for the edifying of the body of Christ*" (v. 12). What is the goal of the hand? He continues in Ephesians:

Till we all come to the unity of the faith and of the knowledge of the Son of God, to a perfect man, to the measure of the stature of the fullness of Christ. v.13

The above verse clearly reveals the expansive purpose of the hand of God. The hand graciously opens Heaven's door for God's people so that they can enter into the full knowledge of the Son. They can gain full maturity in the Son. They can receive their complete inheritance of Sonship—to attain to the full stature of the Anointed One.

The five-fold ministry is represented by the five golden pillars that support the first veil. God gave Moses the pattern of the Tabernacle in which it specified five golden pillars at the first veil, combined with four golden pillars at the second veil. The total of nine golden pillars represents the nine gifts of the Spirit. The nine gifts of the Spirit are listed in First Corinthians 12:8-10, as follows:

- The Gift of Wisdom
- The Gift of Knowledge
- The Gift of Faith
- The Gift of Healings
- The Gift of Miracles
- The Gift of Prophecy
- The Gift of Discerning of Spirits
- The Gift of Tongues
- The Gift of Interpretation of Tongues

The nine gifts of the Spirit support the two veils of the Temple. In other words, the gifts of the Spirit empower the Temple ministry. They energize God's hand. They add dynamic power to the Temple experience. And above all, the gifts help verify and confirm the government of God.

Every son and daughter of God who enters the Temple through the first veil with its five pillars will learn to live, move, and operate in the gifts of the Spirit. The gifts are so integral to the Temple that they stand at the openings into both the Holy Place and the Holy of Holies. The gifts are so important in the governmental order of the Temple that they are represented as golden pillars. The opening of the Temple among God's people today will be confirmed and witnessed by the operation of the nine gifts of the Spirit. There is a misconception in the minds of many that the gifts of the Spirit involve strong emotions or dramatic actions. But take notice that the gifts can operate in diverse conditions and are not limited by our human biases. In fact, some gifts such as wisdom, knowledge, faith, and discernment can operate in silence. Other gifts such as healings, miracles, and prophecy will often involve dramatic public impact. The restoration of the Temple and its correspondent gifts will allow all of us to learn the principles of their operation.

Some Christian assemblies teach against spiritual gifts. They often claim that the gifts were only for the virgin Church in the times of the apostles. They deny the rightful place of spiritual gifts in their assemblies. This is serious error. It does injury to the pattern of the Temple, which God provided His people, and it does injustice to the innocent people who are never taught the treasures of the Temple. It means that large portions of Christian assemblies dwell strictly in the court. They are not taught the divine order and government of the Temple and therefore they do not have access to the gifts of the Spirit, which moved powerfully in the virgin Church.

We thank God for the ministers of the court. Their faithfulness and dedication have preserved the elementary teachings of the Scriptures. The spiritual experiences and principles provided in the court are essential in the life of every child of God, and the court ministries have been good stewards in making these provisions. The court ministers, however, can only teach what they have personally experienced. They have not taught the Temple treasures because they have not experienced them. There is no blame to ascribe. It is simply in accordance with the purposes of God that allowed the Temple to be hidden until this new day that now dawns.

We have received the call of God to enter the first veil into the Holy Place. No man can take this honor to himself. It is precisely in accordance with the will and call of God. *"How shall they hear without a preacher? And how shall they preach unless they are sent? As it is written, 'How beautiful are the feet of those who preach the gospel of peace, who bring glad tidings of good things!'"* (Romans 10:14-15).

The God-called men and women of the virgin Church understood both the court and the Temple. It was expected that a child of God who first believed at the gate of the court would then go on to possess the complete gospel of peace. The glad tidings did not stop at the court. The Temple was open through the administration of divine government and the people—filled with the zeal of the Lord of hosts—urged one another to go on to maturity in the Temple treasures of the Son. They understood that the government was upon His shoulders and that He was the source of their spiritual power. Their testimony was fired by conviction: "*Of the increase of His government and peace there will be no end*" (Isaiah 9:7).

The Temple treasures have never gone away. They can be ignored, and they can be spoken against by court ministers who honestly do not comprehend the Temple. But ignorance and opposition do not change the fact that our inheritance in Christ includes His spiritual Temple. The Temple can never be disannulled or destroyed for it consists of heavenly substance. It is the substance of the Spirit and the Word, which even now are translating God's people out of the court-only mentality into the Temple reality. The spiritual fire of Temple ministry will ignite revival across America and around the world. It will be a revival of both the court and the Temple in all of their combined potency and purity.

Let this prayer of the apostles live again in the hearts of the Lord's people.

> *"Grant to Your servants that with all boldness they may speak Your word, by stretching out Your hand to heal, and that signs and wonders may be done through the name of Your holy Servant Jesus."* ACTS 4:29-30

Stretch out your mighty hand, O Father. Let the presence of your divine government be made known. Let the first veil with its five golden pillars be established in the hearts of your people. Omnipotent Father, cause your Word to be spoken with boldness. Let the golden pillars of the Temple be revealed with healings, miracles, signs and wonders done in the name of the Lord. Let the nine gifts of the Spirit be fully expressed as your governmental order is exalted.

DIVINE GOVERNMENT: I NOW UNDERSTAND.
HUMBLY I BOW TO MY FATHER'S COMMAND.

THE SHOWBREAD

Key Words: Teachings of Truth

Significance

The showbread signifies truth. It is referred to in the New Testament in the following terms: the living bread, the mind of Christ, the doctrine of Christ, and the apostles' doctrine. In essence, it is the unadulterated Word of God. The showbread edifies the human soul with the elemental teachings of God's Kingdom. Showbread supplies the divine principles upon which the court and the Temple can be firmly established.

Supportive Scriptures

The entrance of Your words gives light; it gives understanding to the simple. PSALM 119:130

Jesus said, "I am the bread of life. He who comes to me shall never hunger." JOHN 6:35

"Give us this day our daily bread." MATTHEW 6:11

And they continued steadfastly in the apostles' doctrine and fellowship, in the breaking of bread, and in prayers. ACTS 2:42

Let this mind be in you which was also in Christ Jesus. PHILIPPIANS 2:5

We have the mind of Christ. 1 CORINTHIANS 2:16

Physical Description

The showbread table was made of acacia wood overlaid with pure gold. The table was three feet long, one-and-one-half feet wide, and two-and-one-fourth feet in height. The top edge of the table had a gold border, crown, or molding. Each of the four corners of the table had a gold ring to hold the two gold-covered staves used to transport the table. The tools and utensils used to make the bread were made of gold: dishes, spoons, bowls, and covers—all of pure gold. (See Exodus 25:23-30; 37:10-16.)

Upon entering the first veil into the Tabernacle, the location of the table would be on one's right (the north) side. (See Exodus 40:22.)

The actual showbread was made of unleavened wheat flour. Twelve loaves were baked at one time, and these were arranged on the table in two rows of six loaves each. (See Leviticus 24:6.) It is interesting to note there are sixty-six books in the Bible—typified by the two rows of showbread: six and six.

Instructions were given so that the bread would be properly made. There was also a prescribed order in the arrangement of the showbread on the table.

You shall take fine flour and bake twelve cakes with it. Two-tenths of an ephah shall be in each cake. You shall set them in two rows, six in a row, on the pure gold table before the LORD. And you shall put pure frankincense on each row, that it may be on the bread for a memorial, an offering made by fire to the LORD. Every Sabbath he shall set it [the showbread] ***in order*** *before the LORD continually.... And it shall be for Aaron and his sons,* *and they shall eat it in a holy place....* LEVITICUS 24:5-9, EMPHASIS ADDED

Spiritual Application

The truth, which Jesus taught the apostles, is available as pure unleavened showbread in the Holy Place. The passing of two thousand years has not aged the bread of life because it is of spiritual substance. This is not bread that can be corrupted by age. It is not subject to mold or decay or any negative earthly force. It is spiritual manna available in heavenly places in Christ, in the Anointing. It is the Word of God that lives and abides forever. The Savior declared that His Words are Spirit and life. These attributes of everlasting Spirit and incorruptible life make His showbread very desirable.

Teachings of truth will transform the mind and heart of every recipient. The people of God rejoice in the knowledge of the truth because it brings liberty from all oppression. The beauty and power contained in the teachings of the Son of God are truly astonishing. "*...the people were astonished at His teaching*" (Matthew 7:28).

His teaching! It is a Temple treasure whose value is inestimable. Notice that the showbread is carefully presented on a table overlaid with gold, and all vessels belonging to the table are made of pure gold. Near the showbread table is the golden candlestick whose seven golden flames illumine the gold of the table. Gold represents righteousness. Consider the pattern: unleavened bread is presented in a golden environment. The emphasis is upon the absolute purity and righteousness of His Word.

Recall that the Word of God has application and purpose in the court. All of God's people are required to cleanse themselves in the water of the Word in the laver. In fact, the Word of God is integral within every court vessel and office. The court vessels, however, are made of brass, not gold. Brass indicates good value, and it does have its own glory and beauty, yet it is far inferior to the gold found only in the Temple. That is to say, the showbread in the Holy Place possesses greater purity, it expresses the righteousness of the Father and Son more succinctly, and it establishes an order of divine government much higher than the Word found in the court.

Profoundly, the showbread is encompassed by the nine gifts of the Spirit: the five golden pillars at the first veil are combined with the four golden pillars at the second veil. The showbread abides in a room whose golden walls reflect golden-hued light from the golden candlestick. This is the pattern God gave to Moses. It is a pattern that gives the showbread a highly featured position.

We need to analyze the pattern. It has real meaning only when applied to our personal lives. We are the Temple. The showbread should be in a featured position in our daily walk with God. The showbread should be made fresh on a weekly basis and we ought to feed on the showbread daily. Obviously, we are not dealing with literal loaves of bread. This comparison of literal bread in a natural Tabernacle with spiritual bread in a spiritual Temple is evocative. The showbread is no longer the domain of the Aaronic priesthood under the Old Covenant of Law. That was simply the type-and-shadow, or the pattern. Its intent was that God's anointed people would comprehend their inheritance in Christ. The Son fulfilled the Law Covenant and exceedingly surpassed it with the New Covenant of grace and truth. The formalized, ritualized Aaronic priesthood under the Law gave way to the priesthood of all believers who abide above the Law in the faith and life of the Son.

The Son washed us from our sins in His own blood; more than this, He also made us to be kings and priests unto God the Father. To believe in the Son is salvation, and yet our new birth yields ever-greater benefits and blessings. Indeed, He has called and chosen us to be a royal priesthood who will enter the Temple to feed upon the showbread. The showbread is the mind of Christ revealed in man. The showbread table in the

Holy Place presents the wisdom and knowledge of God in a context that we can assimilate. Here, in the Holy Place, there is an ever-present abundance of fresh bread.

Ironically, and quite sadly, much of humanity is starving for the true bread of life. The Christian ministry offers the court to humanity, but the court does not sufficiently satisfy the spiritual hunger. Always remember that the showbread is not made nor dispensed in the court. The showbread table with its truth doctrine is a crucial part of the inheritance due those who believe in the Son, and we must enter the Holy Place to partake of it.

The Son introduced a spiritual Temple governed by a spiritual priesthood who function according to a spiritual order, the Order of Melchizedek. All believers are baptized into the Melchizedek Order, though this is seldom taught to the family of God. We must know that Jesus is the High Priest of the Melchizedek Order and every believer is baptized into Jesus Christ. We are members of His Body, and Melchizedek is the name of our eternal order. We are born again through faith in the Son of God and we are to grow up in Him in all things.

We need to fervently embrace our heritage in Christ. Every believing soul has entered the Melchizedek Order and has full access not only to the showbread table but all aspects of the Temple. What dramatic transitions were brought to pass by the change of Covenants! Under the Old Law Covenant, the Aaronic priesthood was limited to a select few. They alone had access to the showbread. They alone had the right to enter the Temple. The Aaronic Order was very exclusive and restrictive. In brilliant contrast, the New Covenant of grace and truth established the Melchizedek Order. Every believer is born into the Melchizedek Order when they enter the court through the gate of faith. Entrance into the court provides every believer with the opportunity to enter the Holy Place to partake of the showbread.

In the Aaronic Order the priesthood was strictly limited to the tribe of Levi—one tribe out of twelve—and only the elite of Levi were appointed to the priesthood. The Melchizedek Order, however, opened the gate of opportunity to all of humanity. Great men and women of faith could arise from every walk of life and from every nation. God so loved the world that He gave His Son. Whosoever believes in the Son is saved. Whosoever will—let him drink of the water of life freely. Come unto Me all who labor and are heavy laden.

The Savior initiated this major shift in orders. He was not born of the tribe of Levi. He was not trained or educated by a traditional religious institution. Both He and His apostles failed to fit into the acceptable mold of the old religious order of the Sadducees and Pharisees. The Aaronic Order, based on exclusive natural birthright, was overwhelmed by the Melchizedek Order, based on divine election. It is startling to realize that only a few priests of the tribe of Levi, and never a woman, ever entered into the beauteous hidden chambers of the Tabernacle. Only the elite of the Aaronic priesthood ever tasted of the showbread.

The twelve loaves of showbread, available for all of God's people, are essential for proper spiritual growth. The number twelve represents governmental perfection. There were twelve tribes of Israel, twelve loaves of showbread, twelve apostles, and twelve foundations in the New Jerusalem. "*The wall of the city had twelve foundations, and in them the names of the twelve apostles of the Lamb*" (Revelation 21:14, KJV). The apostles' names—that is, their character, their understanding, their doctrine—are in the twelve foundations. We must conclude that the teachings of truth given by the Lamb to the apostles are foundational in the life of every believer. Only the truth doctrine can establish the foundational underpinnings of the Temple. Only the showbread can explain the broad ramifications of the Melchizedek Order.

The showbread provides weighty spiritual instruction. It is this instruction that is referenced as the doctrine of Christ, or the apostles' doctrine. *Doctrine*, a term used extensively throughout the New Testament, simply means instruction. The twelve loaves of showbread represent the instruction of truth given by the Son to His twelve apostles. In turn, they gave this bread to the world. The bread of life is not nationalistic in either origin or destiny. It does not come to us in a bread wrapper bearing a denominational or religious label. It is not made of earthly ingredients. The bread of life is the Father's gift from Heaven and it brings liberty to all mankind.

Nothing in either the natural or spiritual domains can be established without proper instruction. Proper instruction lays the necessary foundation. Instruction in the knowledge of the truth must be provided if the Temple is to be established among mankind. A vast preponderance of this divine instruction is found at the showbread table. How vital is this form of instruction!

> *Give instruction to a wise man, and he will be still wiser; teach a just man, and he will increase in learning.*
> PROVERBS 9:9

> *He who disdains instruction despises his own soul....*
> PROVERBS 15:32

The Son freely gave the bread of life to humanity. He emphasized that the doctrine He taught came from the Father. "*My doctrine is not Mine, but His* [the Father] *who sent Me* [the Son]" (John 7:16). The Son spoke the Word received from the Father. It is this Word—written eternally in the fabric of the character of both the Father and Son—which is represented by the showbread.

The showbread dwells in the light of the candlestick. That is, the truth doctrine exists in the light of the Spirit. Candlestick and showbread: Spirit and truth. The doctrine is not a dead formula. To know the doctrine is to be instructed by the Word of God in the Spirit.

> *"Man shall not live by bread alone, but by* ***every word that proceeds from the mouth of God."*** MATTHEW 4:4, EMPHASIS ADDED

> *"Give us this day* ***our daily bread.*** MATTHEW 6:11, EMPHASIS ADDED

> ***"I am the bread of life.... If anyone eats of this bread, he will live forever; and the bread that I shall give is My flesh, which I shall give for the life of the world."*** JOHN 6:48, 51, EMPHASIS ADDED

> *Jesus took* ***bread,*** *blessed and broke it, and* ***gave it to the disciples and said, "Take, eat; this is My body."*** MATTHEW 26:26, EMPHASIS ADDED

> *The bread which we break, is it not the communion of* ***the body of Christ? For we, though many, are one bread and one body; for we all partake of that one bread.*** 1 CORINTHIANS 10:16-17, EMPHASIS ADDED

The above Scriptures show the progression of the bread—the doctrine of Christ—from the individual Savior to the salvation of the world. It began with the Savior. The Word was made flesh and dwelt among men. During this time of His human ministry, the Son alone possessed the bread of life. He gave the bread to the apostles through daily instruction for three-and-one-half years, and on the Day of Pentecost the bread began to truly live in the apostles. They became the Temple of God among mankind. In turn, the apostles instructed multitudes so that they could also partake of the bread of life. The declaration of the pure Word of God mightily impacted the history of the human family. Wisely, the Father inspired the compilation of the biblical record in order to preserve the instruction—the doctrine—the bread—the truth—which came down from Heaven.

The references to the doctrine of Christ are many and some are included here so that every seeker will realize the great importance of the showbread table. Please prayerfully consider the vital role of truth doctrine in the Temple.

The Jewish authorities took the apostles captive and accused them:

> *"...look, **you have filled Jerusalem with your doctrine,** and intend to bring this Man's blood on us!" But Peter and the other apostles answered and said: "We ought to obey God rather than men."* ACTS 5:28-29, EMPHASIS ADDED

The apostles were Temple vessels whose words possessed power. Their expression of the showbread was witnessed by gifts of the Spirit (the nine golden pillars), the illumination of the Spirit (the candlestick), and the authority of divine government (the first veil). The apostles' doctrine was the same Word of truth spoken by the Son. The Temple of the Son manifested healings, miracles, signs, and wonders not only in the individual firstborn Son, but also in the collective Temple of His Body. The power of the Spirit accompanied the authority of the Word. This unique Temple blend of Spirit and Word is called the *Logos*. *Logos* expresses the life and character of the Father and Son. Multitudes received the *Logos* as the Temple was revealed to humanity. All who received the *Logos* were made partakers of the unsearchable riches of Christ.

The Apostle Paul counted all of his prideful human identity as lost compared to the spiritual riches he found in the Temple of the Son. Paul understood the Temple not made by hands. He received revelatory insight in the Holy of Holies and placed this hidden manna upon the showbread table so that all of God's family could partake of it. Paul loved to make the showbread. Often he referred to the bread of life as the *doctrine*.

> *You obeyed from the heart that form of doctrine to which you were delivered.* ROMANS 6:17

There was a form, or a proper ordering, of the showbread table. Paul became a master of it. To him the bread represented the precious life of Christ—an anointed Word—the *Logos*. The teachings of the Savior and the apostles were never intended to be a code of dead letter rules and regulations. To them the Spirit of the Word mattered most. Their teachings were carried on the wings of faith and love. The Spirit of resurrection life energized the Word of God spoken from the Temple.

The showbread table has such vital importance in the Temple because the instruction of truth establishes the pure foundations of the court and Temple. The truth spoken in love brings liberty from any form of error, deceit, leaven, hypocrisy, or false doctrine. Only the truth removes earthly religious barriers so the people of God are free to enter their full inheritance in the Father and Son.

> *Therefore let us keep the feast, not with old leaven, nor with the leaven of malice and wickedness, but with the unleavened bread of sincerity and truth.* 1 CORINTHIANS 5:8

The history of earthly religion has too often been a sad display of malice and wickedness. We, the human family, have learned through the things we have suffered. Now we are ready to move into a great new day wherein the unleavened bread of sincerity and truth becomes our daily manna.

Mature sons and daughters of God visit the showbread table on a daily basis. They sustain themselves with the bread of life. They recognize the showbread as the doctrine of Christ—His instructions. They personally experience an inner transformation in their character.

The truth doctrine is a central treasure in the Temple, and the world awaits the full expression of this living Word. It is God's will that all mankind can be... *nourished in the words of faith and of the good doctrine which you have carefully followed ... give attention to reading, to exhortation, to doctrine.... Take heed to yourself and to the doctrine. Continue in them, for in doing this you will save both yourself and those who hear you.* (1 Timothy 4:6, 13, 16)

The Aaronic priests of the Mosaic Tabernacle were told by God to eat the showbread. The right to eat the showbread was part of their priestly domain, or inheritance. We are to follow this pattern. We are to eat the bread of life consistently, diligently. We are to partake of the doctrine of Christ—the showbread, the *Logos*—as part of our daily spiritual diet. The Master has spoken His instructions:

"*I am the bread of life.*" John 6:35

"*Take, eat....*" Matthew 26:26

Instructed in truth: I can now express
The mind of Christ and His righteousness.

continue in the word

THE GOLDEN CANDLESTICK

Key Words: Divine Illumination

Significance

The golden candlestick signifies the sevenfold expression of the Spirit of God. It is the illumination of the human soul by the indwelling Holy Spirit. The pure gold of the seven lamps of the candlestick is symbolic: Gold means the righteousness of God, and seven represents divine completion. The fact that the candlestick is the only source of light in the Holy Place indicates our complete reliance on the Spirit when we enter the Temple.

Supportive Scriptures

> *"I am the light of the world. He who follows Me shall not walk in darkness, but have the light of life."* JOHN 8:12

> *You will light my lamp; the* LORD *my God will enlighten my darkness.* PSALM 18:28

> *Arise, shine; for your light has come! And the glory of the Lord is risen upon you … the* LORD *will be to you an everlasting light, and your God your glory.* ISAIAH 60:1,19

The light of the gospel of the glory of Christ, who is the image of God, should shine on them. For we do not preach ourselves, but Christ Jesus the Lord.... 2 CORINTHIANS 4:4-5

If we walk in the light as He is in the light, we have fellowship with one another, and the blood of Jesus Christ His Son cleanses us from all sin ... and truly our fellowship is with the Father and with His Son Jesus Christ. 1 JOHN 1:7, 3

Physical Description

The candlestick was formed of pure gold. It consisted of a main shaft with six side branches, or arms, three on each side. Each of the six side branches had three almond-shaped bowls with decorative knops (knobs) and flowers. The main shaft had four almond-shaped bowls with its knops and flowers. Seven lamps are specified. (See Exodus 25:37; 37:23; Numbers 8:2.)

Notice that the main shaft of the candlestick had four sets of bowls, knobs, and flowers whereas each of the six side branches had three sets. The main shaft, as we will soon discover, represents the Spirit of the Lord—His absolute authority. Any combination of a side branch with the main shaft would equal seven sets of bowls, knobs, and flowers. Seven means completion.

Several gold utensils were associated with the candlestick: tongs, snuff dishes, and oil vessels. (See Numbers 4:9; Exodus 25:38; 37:23.) Pure olive oil fueled the candlestick.

And you [Moses] *shall command the children of Israel that they bring you pure oil of pressed olives for the light, to cause the lamp to burn continually.* EXODUS 27:20

The Aaronic priests tended the candlestick in the morning and evening. (See Exodus 27:21; 30:8.) The candlestick was located in the Holy Place of the Tabernacle to the left (the south) of the showbread table. (See Exodus 40:24.)

The arrangement of the seven lamps was carefully specified in the Lord's instructions to Moses.

> *And the* L*ORD spoke to Moses, saying: "Speak to Aaron, and say to him, 'When you arrange the lamps, the seven lamps shall give light in front of the lampstand.'" And Aaron did so; he arranged the lamps to face toward the front of the lampstand.* NUMBERS 8:1-3

The emphasis is toward the front, not behind. This indicates a progressive leading of the Spirit in one's life.

The golden candlestick exuded exquisite beauty.

> *Now this workmanship of the lampstand was hammered gold; from its shaft to its flowers it was hammered work.* ***According to the pattern which the LORD had shown Moses, so he made the lampstand.*** NUMBERS 8:4, EMPHASIS ADDED

In other words, the physical form of the candlestick replicated the pattern shown by the Lord.

Spiritual Application

The seven lamps upon the golden candlestick are representative of the sevenfold Spirit of God. The Bible explicitly defines the candlestick:

> *Seven lamps of fire were burning before the throne, which are the seven Spirits of God.* REVELATION 4:5

The seven lamps are *the seven Spirits of God.* Keeping in mind that the seven lamps together made one candlestick, we can discern the seven Spirits of God to be seven distinct expressions of one Spirit. This is a critical point. There are not seven separate Spirits of God, but rather there is one Spirit with seven profound expressions. "*There is ... one Spirit*" (Ephesians 4:4). In this same passage we are urged to "*keep the unity of the Spirit*" (v. 3).

The symbolic design of the golden candlestick conveys the concept of seven distinct expressions, or manifestations, of one Spirit. These seven expressions of the Holy Spirit are listed in Isaiah 11:2, as follows:

- Spirit of the Lord (authority)
- Spirit of Wisdom
- Spirit of Understanding
- Spirit of Counsel
- Spirit of Might (power)
- Spirit of Knowledge
- Spirit of the Fear of the Lord (reverence)

These seven function together in perfect unity and yet each expresses a unique aspect of spiritual enlightenment. The expression of any particular lamp, or Spirit, is always in combination with the lamp of the main shaft, which is the Spirit of the Lord. In all things the Son has preeminence. There is no expression of the Spirit separate from the authority of the Son. For example, an expression of the Spirit of wisdom will be in perfect unity with the Spirit of the Lord—and this combination equals seven bowls, knobs, and flowers. That is, the expression of God's Spirit is always a seven—the perfect unity found only in the Son.

The Father makes His light known through the revelation of His Son, and it is important to realize that we do not experience all of the light at once in a sudden burst of revelation. To the contrary, the Spirit fosters continual growth as we gradually emerge into our full inheritance. There is a gradual unfolding of the light as we continue to explore the riches of the Temple.

The seven lamps of the spiritual candlestick are always burning, yet each seeker must learn to abide in the light as He is in the light. This is a process of maturity. The candlestick directs its light in front of us so we can keep moving forward.

The glory of the mystery of the Gospel of Jesus Christ is that He, the Anointed One, dwells in our hearts by faith. We possess the full inheritance of God in Christ in our new birth. The Anointed One takes up His abode in His people by the presence of His Spirit. This vital principle of the indwelling Christ is much quoted and much discussed. But our true recognition of its reality will indeed translate us out of the court into the Temple. Only in the Temple do we receive the pure, direct light of the candlestick.

The mystery of the indwelling Christ-life can be summed up as *"Christ in you, the hope of glory"* (Colossians 1:27), and yet the Christ, the hope, and the glory are so exceedingly profound that the Heaven of heavens cannot contain their radiance. The Son of God is revealed as the Light of God: *"In Him was life, and the life was the light of men.... That was the true Light which gives light to every man coming into the world"* (John 1:4, 9). Jesus Christ, the Anointed Savior, is the light of every man as far as God is concerned. In God's plan of the ages all mankind will eventually find their true identity and purpose in the light of the Son. Jesus plainly stated it: *"I am the light of the world ... the light of life"* (John 8:12). *"I have come as a light into the world...."* (John 12:46). The light is for the whole world, but the real wonder is that the light makes its abode in our personal Temple. It is good news that the light of the world is the inheritance of mankind on an individual basis.

The Son, as the express image of the Father, possesses the light of the Father. They—Father and Son—take up their abode in the heart of every believer. *"I* [the Son] *in them, and You* [the Father] *in Me; that they may be made perfect in one..."* (John 17:23). *"At that day you will know that I am in My Father, and you in Me, and I in you"* (John 14:20). *"We* [Father and Son] *will come to him* [the believer] *and make Our home with him*" (John 14:23). The light of the Father is the life of His Son, and this life now dwells in us. We have been dignified as heirs of salvation with rightful inheritance in the Son. In process of time we shall learn to exercise the completeness of our inheritance.

Our focus here is the golden candlestick of the Holy Place. It is true that the grace, light, and ministry of the Father and Son bless the court. However, the brilliant core of the fire and light of the Father and Son are found in the Temple. The candlestick is the manifestation of the fire and light of the Spirit. It is the realm of divine illumination. It is the dimension of divine intelligence. God reveals His divine intelligence to those who learn to abide in the Temple of His presence. God has set His seven lamps "*...on a lampstand, that those who enter may see the light. For nothing is secret that will not be revealed, nor anything hidden that will not be known and come to light*" (Luke 8:16-17). We must enter the Temple to behold the light.

The seven lamps of divine illumination yield their golden glow within the Holy Place beside the showbread table. This is a reality for those who have girded their minds, focused their vision, and humbled their self-will to the will of God in order to enter the first veil into the Temple. The Father desires that His people awaken to their Temple treasures. "*For where your treasure is, there your heart will be also*" (Luke 12:34). As long as a person knows only the court, then the court will be his only treasure. His heart, therefore, will abide in the court never realizing that the greatest treasures abide within the Temple.

Our vision needs to be sharpened and our hope increased. Christ is not limited to the court. We must come to this awareness of hidden treasures within the Temple: "*...the knowledge of **the mystery of God, both of the Father and of Christ, in whom are hidden all the treasures of wisdom and knowledge***" (Colossians 2:2-3, emphasis added). These special treasures will never be found in the court. The revelation of the treasures of wisdom and knowledge is not the purpose of the court, but is reserved for those who desire to go on to perfection, or maturity.

The following Scripture should help shake people loose from all forms of religious bondage to claim their full inheritance:

> *In Him* [the Son] *dwells all the fullness of the Godhead bodily; and you are complete in Him, who is the head of all principality and power.* COLOSSIANS 2:9-10

These anointed words of truth declare that we are *complete in Him*—that is, the firstborn Son who possesses the fullness of the Godhead. This makes the Son to be head over all principalities and powers in Heaven or in Earth. Our completeness is in the Son according to the divine decree of the Father. Therefore, nothing can add or detract from our completeness, or inheritance, in Christ. The small-mindedness of earthly religion will generally try to minimize our inheritance by offering substitutes and diversions, or by emphasizing our human limitations rather than our completeness in Him. The called-out people of the Lord must set their eyes, their vision, yea, their hope, on the treasures that are only known as we follow on to know the Lord in His Temple. The Son is the Temple, and we are complete in Him.

The carnal mind tries to cheat God's people out of their Temple treasures by insinuating that the promises of God recorded in the Bible are too great and we ought to settle for something far less. The carnal mind often exerts its subtle influence through earthly religion. Always remember that the carnal mind is at enmity with God. Carnal-mindedness and spiritual illumination are mortal enemies. The natural, carnal, self-willed mind of man cannot perceive spiritual wisdom and knowledge. We must not allow carnality in any form—even in the guise of religion—to cheat us of our spiritual heritage. *"Beware lest anyone cheat you through philosophy and empty deceit, according to the tradition of men, according to the b... ic principles of the world, and not according to Christ"* (Colossians 2:8).

According to the teachings of Christ we ought to enter the Temple to receive illumination from the golden candlestick:

> *Let your loins be girded about, and **your lights*** [lamps] ***burning.*** LUKE 12:35, KJV, EMPHASIS ADDED

To have our loins girded means we have properly progressed through the court to enter the Temple. In here, in the Holy Place, our lights are burning because God's sevenfold Spirit is expressing His manifold riches. From our newfound position in the Holy Place, we can look upon the court with keen appreciation and understanding. We recognize the court as a wonderful operation of the grace of God in its provision of elementary salvation and deliverance. The court is not to be despised. Its foundational operations are essential, never to be lost or forgotten. Yet God's mighty Spirit urges His people today to explore the treasures revealed in the light of the golden candlestick.

Let the Holy Spirit speak through the following verse:

> *That God, the God of our Lord Jesus Christ, and the all-glorious Father, will give you spiritual wisdom and the insight to know more of him: that you may receive that inner illumination of the spirit which will make you realize how great is the hope to which he is calling you—the magnificence and splendor of the inheritance promised to Christians—and how tremendous is the power available to us who believe in God.* EPHESIANS 1:17-19, PH

The meaning of these words leaps from the page: *spiritual wisdom, insight, inner illumination, the hope, the inheritance*, and *the power*. Paul, an heir of the Temple, wrote these words to describe the treasures he had found. His prayer and hope was that God's people would also discover the unsearchable riches available in Christ.

Paul, along with the other apostles, always endeavored to establish the believers in both the court and the Temple. The apostles understood both realms, and they realized that the court and the Temple go together. The Son, as the prototype, was the Apostle and High Priest of our profession. He demonstrated the harmonious structure of the court and the Temple. The Savior moved among the people with compassion and pity. He ministered to their needs with spiritual discernment. He was the master of the court, the Holy Place, and the Holy of Holies, and He was abundantly able to minister from each realm as the need required.

It was God who gave Moses the pattern in which the Temple existed inside the court. Take careful notice: The Temple exists in the presence of the court. Conversely, the court does not exist as a separate entity unto itself. In fulfillment of the pattern provided by the Father, the Son was master of both the court and the Temple.

Court and Temple: this was the heavenly pattern revealed in the Son. It is an elemental concept that needs to sink deeply into our spiritual consciousness. The Son established His apostles in both the court and the Temple and this made them great in God. The apostles simply replicated the spiritual blueprint spoken and demonstrated by the Savior. They established multitudes of disciples who experienced their own spiritual maturity by personal entrance into both the court and the Temple. This elect company of mature overcomers emerged from the virgin Church to become our spiritual forefathers. We are grateful to God for the honorable and righteous men and women He ordained to establish the pure foundations for all following generations. Our spiritual heritage—a sure foundation of both the court and the Temple—will be restored in this new day.

The light of the golden candlestick in the Holy Place revealed abundant treasure. Overwhelmed by the joyous realization of the Temple treasures, the apostles announced the good news they received from the Son. In essence, they declared:

The heavens are open!
The Temple is open!
Approach the throne of grace with boldness!

You were once darkness, but now you are light in the Lord. Walk as children of light. EPHESIANS 5:8

Ye are all the children of light, and the children of the day.... 1 THESSALONIANS 5:5, KJV

"*You are the light of the world.*" MATTHEW 5:14

...among whom you shine as lights in the world. PHILIPPIANS 2:15

The Aaronic priest in the court received natural light from the sun and moon, but inside the Tabernacle he depended on the light of the candlestick. The true light expressed through the Son to the apostles, and then to multitudes of disciples, was the golden candlestick. Its sevenfold expression was the source of divine illumination available in the Temple of the Son.

Today in the Melchizedek Order we receive this same divine light. We, too, are heirs of the Temple of the Son—and therefore we are heirs of the candlestick. It is a light far greater than any natural source:

The sun shall no longer be your light by day, nor for brightness shall the moon give light to you; but the LORD will be to you an everlasting light, and your God your glory. ISAIAH 60:19

The city had no need of the sun or of the moon to shine in it, for the glory of God [the Father] *illuminated it. The Lamb* [the Son] *is its light.* REVELATION 21:23

The light of the knowledge of the glory of the Father is revealed through His Son in the lives of His people. This is our inheritance of light in the Lord. It is a Temple condition, a heavenly kingdom, and a spiritual city wherein we can abide in the illumined presence of immortality.

IN THE HOLY SPIRIT THE SON IS MADE KNOWN:
HIS SEVEN LAMPS OF FIRE BURN BEFORE THE THRONE.

[illegible]

[illegible]

The light of the knowledge of the g[illegible] of the [illegible] [illegible] [illegible] people. [illegible]

[illegible]

[illegible]

Complete reliance upon the Holy Spirit

THE GOLDEN ALTAR

Key Words: Prayer and Praise

Significance

The golden altar signifies the purest essence of worship. It is total consecration unto God in the holiness of His presence. The prayers and praises of the people—anointed with the power of resurrection life—ascend to God from the deepest recesses of the soul.

Supportive Scriptures

> *Give unto the LORD the glory due to His name; worship the Lord in the beauty of holiness.* PSALM 29:2

> *Oh, worship the LORD in the beauty of holiness!* PSALM 96:9

> *Let my prayer be set before You as incense, the lifting up of my hands as the evening sacrifice.* PSALM 141:2

> *We are the circumcision, who worship God in the Spirit, rejoice in Christ Jesus, and have no confidence in the flesh.* PHILIPPIANS 3:3

> *Blessing and honor and glory and power be to Him who sits on the throne, and to the Lamb, forever and ever!* REVELATION 5:13

Physical Description

The golden altar was made of acacia wood overlaid with pure gold. Quite small in size compared to the brazen altar in the court, the golden altar was one-and-one-half feet square and stood three feet in height. The top of the altar was edged with a golden crown, and each of the four corners had a golden horn.

> *You shall make an altar to burn incense on; you shall make it of acacia wood.... you shall overlay its top, its sides all around, and its horns with pure gold; and you shall make for it a molding* [border or crown] *of gold all around.* EXODUS 30:1, 3

The sides of the altar had gold rings and gold-covered wood staves to be used in transporting it. It is of notable interest that all vessels of the court and Temple were designed for ease of transportation. It was made for a people who were willing to move as God moved.

The golden altar was strategically located directly in front of the inner veil, which separated the Holy Place from the Holy of Holies. *"You shall put it before the veil that is before the ark of the Testimony..."* (Exodus 30:6).

Daily incense was to be burned upon the golden altar. *"Aaron shall burn on it sweet incense every morning.... And when Aaron lights the lamps* [candlestick] *at twilight, he shall burn incense on it..."* (Exodus 30:7-8). Ingredients for the incense were carefully defined. *"The LORD said to Moses: 'Take sweet spices, stacte and onycha and galbanum, and pure frankincense with these sweet spices; there shall be equal amounts of each. You shall make of these an incense...'"* (Exodus 30:34-35). The emphasis was on purity, sweetness, and uniqueness.

"...the pure incense of sweet spices, according to the work of the apothecary [the maker of perfumed compounds]" (Exodus 37:29, KJV).

The burning of this unique incense upon the golden altar was imbued with deep significance. The altar was not to be defiled by any other type of offering. *"You shall not offer strange incense on it, or a burnt offering, or a grain offering; nor shall you pour a drink offering on it"* (Exodus 30:9).

Once each year the priest was instructed to bring blood from the brazen altar to be placed upon the four horns of the golden altar. (See Exodus 30:10.) Blood was also taken into the Holy of Holies to be sprinkled on the Mercy Seat. This ritual portrays the spiritual connection that always exists between the brazen altar and the Holy Places within the Temple.

Spiritual Application

The annual ritual in which the priest transferred sacrificial blood from the brazen altar to the golden altar carries wondrous implications. It means that the influence of the Savior's sacrificial death on the Cross remains with us as we progress in the Temple. Our spiritual growth and maturity are forever linked to the Cross. The unity of fellowship between each believer and the Savior can never be broken. Without His death on the Cross, there would be no forgiveness of sin, no spiritual heritage, and no Temple treasures. To emphasize this vital point, God had Moses sprinkle blood from the brazen altar upon the book, the people, the Tabernacle, and all vessels of the ministry. (See Hebrews 9:19-21.)

In accordance with this principle, the Aaronic priest took burning coals from the brazen altar, placed the coals in the golden censer, and carried the censer into the Holy Place of the Tabernacle. Here, on the golden altar, he poured incense over the hot coals within the censer. The sweet odor of the burning incense filled the entire Tabernacle. This symbolic action provides another strong link between the work of the

Cross and our spiritual offering of prayer and praise unto God. The compound of the spices used in making the incense was specific and its sole usage was confined to the golden altar. Any other mixture of spices, or any other type of offering, was forbidden. Anything other than the pure incense was considered as strange fire.

God does not desire strange fire. There is an acceptable approach to Him. As far as God is concerned there is a sweet, wholesome fragrance in our lives. It is the fragrance of Christ within us. (See 2 Corinthians 2:15.) It is the Christ, the Anointing, within the lives of His people that is pleasing to God. For anyone to think they can approach the Holy of Holies with folly in their heart—or guile, or greed, or selfish ambition—they are sadly mistaken. We are indeed to approach the throne of grace with boldness, but this we are able to do only as the Spirit and life of the Son dwells within us.

> *Walk in love, as Christ also has loved us and given Himself for us,* ***an offering and a sacrifice to God for a sweet-smelling aroma.*** EPHESIANS 5:2, EMPHASIS ADDED

Our recognition of the Son of God as Savior and Redeemer is a vital component of the incense of prayer offered at the golden altar. The earnest praise and prayers of the saints, ascending as the pure essence of worship, is like a sweet aroma unto God and His heavenly host. This is a deeper realm of worship than that found in the court. The court worship is typified by brass because human consciousness and human zeal are not only tolerated, but expected. However, the worship in the Temple at the golden altar is typified by gold—the righteousness of God. Self-consciousness and human zeal are mortified by the Spirit as one enters the first veil into the golden atmosphere of the Holy Place.

The Holy Places only exist in the Temple, not the court. Worship in the Temple is governed by the Holy Spirit combined with the zeal of the Lord of hosts. *"Being filled with the fruits of righteousness which are by Jesus Christ, to the glory and praise of God"* (Philippians 1:11). The incense of *glory and praise* offered at the golden altar is described as sweet each time it is mentioned in the Book of Exodus. This term is also used in the New Testament. The aroma released by the burning of the sweet incense in the old Tabernacle must have been wonderful. But the worship of God in the Spirit is sweeter by far.

The golden altar's special essence of worship is due in large measure to its effortlessness. This is a worship that simply flows from the innermost being of one's soul. It is uncontaminated by self-will; it is not a self-effort to please either God or man. The human soul, having drawn near the deepest treasures of the Lord's presence, effortlessly overflows with praise.

> *The temple was filled with smoke from the glory of God and from His power....* REVELATION 15:8

> *Holy, holy, holy is the LORD of hosts; the whole earth* [our earthen vessel] *is full of His glory!* ISAIAH 6:3

Smoke from the burning incense on the golden altar wafted throughout the Mosaic Tabernacle: So also today the glory and power of God's Spirit will fill the Temple of the Son with smoke. Consider the smoke to be the overwhelming influence of God's power and glory within the lives of His Temple people. Our human influence dies out as His divine influence (smoke) takes control.

The golden altar is usually accompanied by an inner condition of great calm and quietude. Sometimes the presence of the Lord's glory and power will calm the physical body into a state of absolute rest. In this profound state of worship, the soul is made abundantly alive in the Spirit. All the faculties and senses of the inner man are sharpened to a keen focus while the awareness of the physical world becomes momentarily subdued.

The inner realm of the golden altar can be experienced either individually or collectively. As a general rule, the golden altar condition is more readily available in a small group situation. The atmosphere of a home meeting—friendly, informal, and comfortable—can often be helpful in gaining deep spiritual consecration. However, large public meetings serve many important functions. Indeed, there were times when the Savior and the apostles spoke to multitudes. Miracles and healings were indeed accomplished in large public gatherings. And yet most meetings among the called-out of the virgin Church were held in the homes of the believers. These home meetings, though small in number, were mighty in the Spirit. Formality and self-consciousness are the spiritually limiting factors in large public meetings. The larger the gathering, the more need there is for control and formality, and hence, more self-consciousness.

In spite of these obstacles, it is possible for individual worshipers in large public meetings to experience the deep realms of the inner Temple. The key is always the same: minimize human distractions by giving total focus of the mind and heart to the Lord. Closing the eyes helps. We must always remember that God is fully capable of helping us overcome every obstacle. He can speak to His people in home meetings, in large public gatherings, or on an individual basis. It is the way in which we approach Him that is important.

> *But at midnight Paul and Silas were praying and singing hymns to God, and the prisoners were listening to them. Suddenly there was a great earthquake, so that the foundations of the prison were shaken; and immediately all the doors were opened and everyone's chains were loosed.* Acts 16:25-26

Paul and Silas had been horribly beaten with rods. Confined to the inner dungeon of the prison, their feet were fastened in stocks. Bruised and bloodied and imprisoned, they approached the throne of God's grace at midnight, the darkest hour. By turning their focus upon God through prayer and singing, they entered the Temple to worship at the golden altar so very near the Holy of Holies.

Prayerfully consider all that was involved in this amazing experience. The inner veil, which covered the Holy of Holies, was rent in two when the Savior died on the Cross. The veil was literally ripped down its center so that the linen curtain fell to the sides to reveal the golden Ark. The Bible informs us that a great earthquake occurred at this time of the Savior's crucifixion. *"Then, behold, the veil of the temple was torn in two from top to bottom; and the earth quaked, and the rocks were split"* (Matthew 27:51). At this critical moment, the Temple was opened forever in Heaven for the human family. The Temple treasures, including the golden Ark in the Holiest, were made available to all who believe. The mighty earthquake signified the shattering of former religious bondages and limitations. The old foundations were moved to make way for the good news of the resurrection morning destined for all men and nations.

Paul and Silas witnessed their own miraculous earthquake that produced three symbolic results: 1) The foundations of the prison were shaken; 2) All prison doors were opened; and 3) Every man's chains were loosed. These three results can be applied to our lives today. When we worship God at the golden altar and discern the rent veil, we will experience the shaking of prison foundations, prison doors will be opened, and chains of bondage will be loosed. Paul and Silas entered the Temple through faithful prayer and singing. They worshipped God at the golden altar and became fully aware of the rent veil. In the Spirit they beheld the Ark of the Covenant with its Mercy Seat and cherubim of glory. Paul and Silas knew that it was imperative for them to go beyond the court into the Temple. They knew it was essential to overcome their negative physical environment—persecution, beatings, prison, chains, and hunger—by exercising their divine inheritance of Temple treasures.

Once they entered the pure worship of the golden altar, they recognized in the Spirit that the veil was rent apart to reveal the Holy of Holies in them. This spiritual realization set the stage for the miraculous earthquake.

In our time, the people of God need to understand their divine inheritance in the Temple. There are many prison foundations—even within Christianity—which must be shaken. Many prison doors need to be opened, and many chains of human bondage need to be loosed. Nothing can accomplish these objectives other than the miraculous force of the Temple treasures. The Father and Son will stand up as Two Witnesses within their people to show forth spiritual treasures. The voice of the Lord will speak in the Temple to those who earnestly seek Him. The gifts of the Spirit will be manifested in the Temple among those who seek out their inheritance in God. Many wondrous demonstrations of divine power, glory, and authority will make us to be eyewitnesses of the majesty of our Savior. In the Temple of the Son, the people will experience unparalleled victory and deliverance.

The people of God will cherish the golden altar when they discover the pure essence of its worship. The power and glory inherent within consecrated prayer and praise will become evident.

> *I heard a voice from the four horns of the golden altar which is before God.* REVELATION 9:13

> *Then another angel, having a golden censer, came and stood at the [golden] altar. He was given much incense, that he should offer it with the prayers of all the saints upon the golden altar which was before the throne. And the smoke of the incense, with the prayers of the*

saints, ascended before God from the angel's hand.
REVELATION 8:3-4

Notice the majestic location of the golden altar in the above Scriptures. It is described as *before God* and also *before the throne*. We are told to approach the throne of grace with boldness. This boldness, the sweet influence of confidence and expectation in God, takes hold of us in the golden altar worship. How effortlessly do we offer up prayers and praise once we sense His glorious presence!

Four golden horns arise from the golden altar in perfect symmetry and balance. Recall that the brazen altar also had four horns. The New Testament provided their meaning: wisdom, righteousness, sanctification (purification), and redemption. Now consider the following verse in regard to the four horns of the golden altar: "*Therefore I exhort first of all that* ***supplications, prayers, intercessions, and giving of thanks*** *be made for all men*" (1 Timothy 2:1, emphasis added). The horns represent four points of emphasis of the golden altar: 1) supplications (petitions and requests; 2) prayers; 3) intercessions (entreaties); and 4) giving of thanks. The sweet Spirit of holiness carries our prayer and praise like incense through the rent veil of the Holy of Holies—unto the very throne of God.

The golden altar possesses immediacy and intimacy with the Holy of Holies because of the rent veil. No longer are the Holy Place and the Holy of Holies divided by the veil. We behold the awesome presence of the golden Ark as we worship at the golden altar. Our prayers and praises ascend as sweet-smelling incense to permeate the entire Temple.

AWAKENED TO THE TREASURES, BORN FROM ABOVE,
MY WORSHIP ASCENDS ON WINGS OF DIVINE LOVE.

PART THREE

The Holy of Holies

Arise, O Lord, to Your resting place,
You and the ark of Your strength.
Let Your priests be clothed with righteousness,
And let Your saints shout for joy.
Psalm 132:8-9

And so, dear brothers,
Now we may walk right into the very Holy of Holies
Where God is, because of the blood of Jesus.
This is the fresh, new, life-giving way
Which Christ has opened up for us
By tearing the curtain—His human body—
To let us into the holy presence of God.
Hebrews 10:19-20, TLB

THE INNER VEIL

Key Words: Open Heavens

Significance

The inner veil, torn in two at the Savior's death, signifies an open entrance into the living presence of God. Direct personal fellowship with the Father is available beyond the rent veil because of the Son's crucifixion and Resurrection.

Supportive Scriptures

"You shall see heaven open, and the angels of God ascending and descending upon the Son of Man." JOHN 1:51

Nevertheless when one turns to the Lord, the veil is taken away. Now the Lord is the Spirit; and where the Spirit of the Lord is, there is liberty. 2 CORINTHIANS 3:16-17

See, I have set before you an open door, and no one can shut it.... He who overcomes, I will make him a pillar in the temple of My God, and he shall go out no more.... REVELATION 3:8, 12

After these things I looked, and behold, a door standing open in heaven.... REVELATION 4:1

Then the temple of God was opened in heaven, and the ark of His covenant was seen in His temple.... REVELATION 11:19

After these things I looked, and behold, the temple of the tabernacle of the testimony in heaven was opened. REVELATION 15:5

Physical Description

The inner veil, also referred to as the second veil, was made of beautifully embroidered linen. It spanned the width of the Tabernacle and hung from the ceiling to the floor. It was approximately eighteen feet in width and fifteen feet in height.

The Old Testament provides the following concise description:

You [Moses] *shall make a veil woven of blue, purple, and scarlet thread, and fine woven linen. It shall be woven with an artistic design of cherubim. You shall hang it upon the four pillars of acacia wood overlaid with gold. Their hooks shall be gold, upon four sockets of silver. And you shall hang the veil from the clasps. Then you shall bring the ark of the Testimony in there, behind the veil.* ***The veil shall be a divider for you between the holy place and the Most Holy.*** EXODUS 26:31-33, EMPHASIS ADDED. (SEE ALSO EXODUS 36:35-36.)

The New Testament offers the following description:

Then indeed, even the first covenant [of Law] *had ordinances of divine service and the earthly sanctuary. For a tabernacle was prepared: the first part, in which*

> *was the lampstand, the table, and the showbread, which is called the sanctuary* [Holy Place]; *and behind* ***the second*** [inner] ***veil,*** *the part of the tabernacle which is called the Holiest of All, which had the golden censer and the ark of the covenant overlaid on all sides with gold....* HEBREWS 9:1-4, EMPHASIS ADDED

Spiritual Application

The inner veil divided the Holy Place from the Holy of Holies for over fifteen hundred years during the old Covenant of Law. The Aaronic priesthood, along with the people of Israel, held the Holy of Holies in awe mingled with fear. The penalty under the Law for any form of violation regarding the Holy of Holies was death. Thus the Holiest was an unknown, and in some respects, fearsome realm. It was established by God in such a way as to be both mystical and forbidding. No one except the appointed priests dared go beyond the veil during the many long centuries leading up to the time of Christ.

The natural linen veil hid the mysterious Ark of the Covenant. It was the sacred persona of the Ark that gave the Holy of Holies its imposing stature. The Ark, veiled from human perception, remained aloof, unknowable, and unapproachable. Thus the veil symbolized the spiritual condition of humanity during the fifteen hundred years of the Law Covenant. It was a condition confined to a natural Tabernacle, which functioned according to a strict, dead letter code of Law.

The Covenant of Law was a veil over human consciousness. The actual veil, with its embroidered wings of the cherubim, was a muted testimony of the glory that was yet to be revealed. The natural Tabernacle held dominion until the Son of God appeared two thousand years ago. Throughout the timeframe of the Law Covenant, humanity could only approach God through the pattern He showed Moses—a pattern constructed of natural substances and governed by a natural priesthood according to ritual, regulation, law, and the literal sacrifice of animals.

The inner veil of the Holy of Holies was ripped down its center at the death of the Savior on the Cross. The dominion of the natural Tabernacle under Law ended at that point in time. The Ark of the Covenant was made available to mankind. Fear and dread fell aside like the rent veil. The golden Ark released a floodtide of grace, truth, mercy, love, and forgiveness as the New Covenant broke forth in the light and power of the resurrected, eternal Son of God.

Today the most significant trait of the inner veil is that it has been permanently ripped open from top to bottom to reveal the golden Ark of the Holiest. We pray the Spirit of God will imprint this image of the rent veil—revealing the Ark of the Covenant—upon the mind of every believer.

> *Then, behold, the veil of the temple was torn in two from top to bottom....* MATTHEW 27:51

> *Then the veil of the temple was torn in two from top to bottom.* MARK 15:38

> *Then the sun was darkened, and the veil of the temple was torn in two.* LUKE 23:45

Our inheritance of the Temple treasures is founded upon the crucifixion and Resurrection of our Savior. He is the Captain of our salvation. He is the Forerunner who opened the way into the Holy of Holies. The veil was torn in two at His crucifixion to clearly show that the way into heavenly places in Christ is open. Our hope to inherit the deepest Temple treasures, founded unfailingly upon the Son, is realized as we pass through the rent veil.

> *This hope we have as an anchor of the soul, both sure and steadfast, and which enters* ***the Presence behind the veil****, where the forerunner has entered for us, even*

Jesus, having become High Priest forever according to the order of Melchizedek. HEBREWS 6:19-20, EMPHASIS ADDED

THE FORERUNNER OPENED THE WAY FOR HUMANITY.
I GO NOW, BEYOND THE VEIL, HIS GLORY TO SEE.

THE GOLDEN ARK

Key Words: God's Heart in Man

Significance

The golden Ark signifies the seat of divine revelation and authority. It is the Spirit-seed of our inheritance in the Son of God. The Ark of the Covenant, the heart of God dwelling in man, is the chief and most precious of all Temple treasures.

Supportive Scriptures

> *Jesus stood and cried out, saying, "If anyone thirsts, let him come to Me and drink. He who believes in Me, as the Scripture has said, out of his heart will flow rivers of living water."* JOHN 7:37-38

> *"Whoever drinks of the water that I shall give him will never thirst. But the water that I shall give him will become in him a fountain of water springing up into everlasting life."* JOHN 4:14

> *Therefore with joy you will draw water from the wells of salvation.* ISAIAH 12:3

"At that day you will know that I am in My Father, and you in Me, and I in you.... If anyone loves Me, he will keep My word; and My Father will love him, and We will come to him and make Our home with him." John 14:20, 23

We have this treasure in earthen vessels, that the excellence of the power may be of God and not of us. 2 Corinthians 4:7

Then the temple of God was opened in heaven, and the ark of His covenant was seen in His temple. And there were lightnings, noises, thunderings, an earthquake, and great hail. Revelation 11:19

Physical Description

The Ark of the Covenant was made of acacia wood overlaid with pure gold both inside and out. This box-like structure was three-and-three-fourths feet in length, two-and-one-fourth feet in width, and two-and-one-fourth feet in height.

And you shall overlay it with pure gold, inside and out you shall overlay it, and shall make on it a molding of gold all around. Exodus 25:11 (See also Exodus 25:10-22; 37:1-9.)

The Ark was designed for ease of transportation. Each of the four upper corners had a gold ring through which the carrying-staves, or poles, were inserted. The two poles—made of acacia wood overlaid with gold—were to remain permanently affixed to the Ark. *"The poles shall be in the rings of the ark; they shall not be taken from it"* (Exodus 25:15). This was a moveable Ark. The twelve tribes of Israel encamped in an orderly arrangement around the Tabernacle. God set a pillar of fire by night, and a pillar of cloud by day, upon the Tabernacle to lead the Israelites through the wilderness. When the pillar moved, the twelve tribes moved with it. The golden Ark, and in fact the entire court and Tabernacle, were quickly dismantled to be physically transported to the next God-appointed destination. This attribute of a moveable Ark holds great spiritual implications.

The Mercy Seat, which covered the Ark, was made of pure gold. Two cherubim, made from the same gold stock used to make the Mercy Seat, emerged from the two ends. The Mercy Seat and the cherubim will be explained in later sections.

The golden Ark contained three items of sacred significance:

1. The golden pot of manna. (See Exodus 16:32-34.)
2. Aaron's rod, which budded. (See Numbers 17:8-10.)
3. The two tablets of stone with the Ten Commandments. (See Exodus 25:16; Deuteronomy 10:2.)

Each of these items adds powerful symbolic weight to the Ark. The Apostle Paul specifically identified them in the New Testament: "*...the ark of the covenant overlaid on all sides with gold, in which were the golden pot that had the manna, Aaron's rod that budded, and the tablets of the covenant*" (Hebrews 9:4). Again, each of these will be explained in the next few sections.

Spiritual Application

The Holy of Holies contained the singular vessel referred to as the Ark of the Covenant. We can appreciate the uniqueness of a room in which there was a single piece of furniture sitting in the center of the room. It was God's own designation that this inner chamber of the Tabernacle was the Holiest. It was not only holy—but indeed it was the Holy of Holies. This term gives recognition to other realms of holiness; that is, there are other realms of spiritual knowledge, awareness, experience, and degrees of divine impartation. But this realm—the Holy of Holies—is ranked by God as supreme because it contains the Ark.

The holiness of the Lord saturates both the court and the Tabernacle. We experience the Lord's holiness even at the gate of faith. Faith in the Son of God is both sacred and holy. The brazen altar, the laver, and Aaron's garments represent various aspects of our spiritual experiences in the court, and they are holy in God's sight.

Then we progress into the Holy Place to participate in ever-deepening realms and dimensions in God. The first veil with its five golden pillars, the showbread table, the golden candlestick, and the golden altar represent the awesome abundance of God's blessings, gifts, promises, inheritance, righteousness—and indeed, holiness. Yet God established the Holy of Holies as the dwelling place of His Ark. All other vessels of the court and Tabernacle are not only supportive of the Ark, but they are dependent upon it. The Ark is the core reason for the existence of the court and Tabernacle. Minus the Ark, the other vessels lose their purpose.

The various components of the Ark hold mysteries of meaning, which we certainly can and should study. But we do so with the understanding that we can only truly know these mysteries when we personally experience them. The Ark, with its vast latent potential, dwells within the Temple of each believer. Yet many of God's people have never experienced the Ark. It is one thing to possess the Ark as hidden potential, but it is far greater when its potential is realized. The Ark is experienced when it is quickened by the gift of Spirit baptism. The same Spirit of God, which raised Christ from the dead, makes its presence known in the very heart of our being.

We learn from the Scriptures that we possess both mind and heart. The heart is more elemental, more instinctive, more innately dominant than the mind, yet both are essential. In a perfected, mature Temple, the mind becomes the Holy Place and the heart becomes the Holy of Holies. Prior to our new birth, we walked according to the passions of the fleshly tabernacle, victimized by the innate self-nature that governed our thinking (mind) and our emotions (heart). Though we were designed through divine intention to become the Temple of God, yet we were dead in trespasses and sins. We were dead to the Spirit but alive to the self-nature. Our mind had no awareness of anything beyond carnal thought. Our heart had no feeling beyond good and evil emotion. Yet in God's appointed season we experienced our new birth in Christ. We were spiritually awakened to our inheritance in the Son. You that were dead He has quickened. Our mind was quickened to truth and our heart was quickened to Spirit.

There are veils of carnality that hold both mind and heart in bondage until we are born from above. The anointing of the Spirit removes the veils of carnal darkness and we begin to see and understand that we are the Temple of God. The following verse specifies the two veils, one over the mind and one over the heart:

> *Their **minds** were blinded. For until this day the same veil remains unlifted in the reading of the Old Testament, because the veil is taken away in Christ. But even to this day, when Moses is read, a veil lies on their **heart. Nevertheless when one turns to the Lord, the veil is taken away.*** 2 CORINTHIANS 3:14-16, EMPHASIS ADDED

In the very next verse Paul pinpoints the Spirit as the key to liberty from the veils over heart and mind. *"Now the Lord is the Spirit, and where the Spirit of the Lord is, there is liberty"* (v. 17). This is a tremendous statement! The Lord *is* the Spirit. Wherever the Spirit of the Lord dwells, there is freedom from carnality. Christ is the Anointing and He dwells in the Temple of His people. Christ, the Anointing, is in you. This is the hope of glory. We need to take the above verse seriously. In Paul's day there were many Israelites who read the Old Testament with a veil over their heart and mind. They read about the

Mosaic Tabernacle and all its fascinating imagery, yet they had no clue as to its spiritual meaning. On the other hand, there were multitudes of believers who received the Spirit of Christ by faith, and in them the veil of carnality was taken away.

In another Scripture Paul makes reference to the "*futility of their mind*" and the "*blindness of their heart*" (see Ephesians 4:17-18). It is reasonable to conclude that every human has both heart and mind. We are presently directing our attention toward the heart in order to establish it as the domain of the Ark. It is the heart that generates human emotion. For every positive emotion there is a correspondent negative emotion. The self-nature of the unregenerate human heart is as a tree of knowledge of good and evil. Yet this fallen tree is transformed into the tree of life when we are born of God. This is a profound study. The main point, which pertains to the present discussion, is to identify the heart with the Ark.

The heart is located in the solar plexus, in the very center and core of our being, what is often referred to as the gut. A "gut reaction" is a term used to describe an instinctive emotional response. The bereaved often say they are "sick at heart." It is often said of someone who exudes great emotional intensity "they have a lot of heart." There are numerous examples, especially in music and poetry, which refer to the heart as the vital center of genuine human emotion. God has promised to write the Law of His divine nature within the heart.

The heart, the solar plexus, and the gut of human emotion—this is the location of the golden Ark once we are born from above as citizens of the kingdom. No longer are we victims of blind emotional urges and compulsions, nor are we seduced by the subtle emotions of the self-nature, but we become overcomers who learn to draw upon the unsearchable riches of Christ in God. Many Christians have never been taught the difference between the mind and the heart. They are unaware of the hidden treasure of the golden Ark within their own solar plexus.

In both the natural and spiritual perspective, the heart is more profoundly dominant than the mind. Naturally speaking, the heart is the source of motivation, inspiration, and emotional energy, which powerfully influence the mind. Even when the emotions of the heart are subdued, they yet exert a pervasive and controlling influence. Spiritually speaking, the Holy of Holies powerfully influences the Holy Place in the same way.

In the following statement by Jesus, He refers to the Ark as the belly:

> *"He that believeth on me, as the scripture hath said, out of his belly [heart] shall flow rivers of living water."*
> JOHN. 7:38, KJV

In other words, the Spirit of resurrection life flows from our innermost being—out of the belly, out of the heart, or out of the Ark of the Temple not made by hands. Jesus wanted His disciples to know the vital importance of the inner Ark of the Covenant, and that they were to experience this miraculous transformation from carnal emotion into the holy presence of divine life. The Savior identified the heart as the primary source of both good and evil in the following verse:

> *"... out of the abundance of the heart the mouth speaks."*
> MATTHEW 12:34

The heart yields abundance continually. Either it is an abundance of carnality unto death, or an abundance of Spirit unto life. It is critical that every believer is enabled to discern their own Temple. Each of us must recognize both the heart and the mind and be able to differentiate between the Holy of Holies and the Holy Place. The Temple treasures increase in their precious content as we progress from the court to the Holy Place and then to the Holiest. Mature sons and daughters of

God have exercised their spiritual senses to discern, appreciate, and properly utilize each spiritual treasure.

The Ark of the Covenant is the heart of the matter. Moses was instructed of God to make the golden Ark first. All other vessels and aspects of the court and Tabernacle came after the Ark. (See Exodus 25:9-16.) The primacy of the Ark was substantiated when the Tabernacle was set up.

> *Then the LORD spoke to Moses, saying: "On the first day of the first month you shall set up the tabernacle of the tent of meeting.* ***You shall put in it the ark of the Testimony,*** *and partition off the ark with the veil."*
> EXODUS 40:1-3, EMPHASIS ADDED

Thus according to the divine pattern, the Ark was the first vessel created and the first vessel set in the Tabernacle. By these examples we can conclude that all other components of the court and Temple are dependent upon the Ark. The golden Ark takes precedence because it is the revelation of God's heart in human temples.

The Tabernacle, including the Ark, was administrated by Aaron and his sons during the time of Moses. This priestly oversight was later extended to the tribe of Levi.

> *At that time the LORD separated the tribe of Levi to bear the ark of the covenant of the LORD, to stand before the LORD to minister unto Him....* DEUTERONOMY 10:8

The other eleven tribes of the Israelites had no part in priestly ministry and were not allowed to bear the Ark. This was the rule and ritual of the Old Law Covenant.

In the New Covenant of grace and truth, the walls of separation between brethren are dissolved. The Ark is no longer an external physical object made of acacia wood overlaid with gold, but it is the living presence of the Father and Son within the human soul. Father and Son have taken up their abode in human temples through the indwelling Spirit. In the solar plexus of our being—in the heart—the Comforter dwells to lead, to guide, to instruct, and to inspire. It is no longer necessary to rely upon an exclusive priesthood to bear the Ark, but we—the called-out people of God—bear the Ark of the New Covenant in Christ.

The natural Ark of the Old Testament was limited by its physical location. There was great concern that it not be lost in war. Apparently it had to be physically present to be effective.

> *Let us bring the ark of the covenant of the* LORD *from Shiloh to us, that when it comes among us it may save us from the hand of our enemies.* 1 SAMUEL 4:3

The Ark's physical presence meant everything because the blessing and power of God abode upon it. The Israelites found much courage to face their enemies when the Ark was near. Its presence caused joy in the hearts of the people.

> *And when the ark of the covenant of the* LORD *came into the camp, all Israel shouted so loudly that the earth shook.* 1 SAMUEL 4:5

Today the Ark is the possession of every believer who is born of the Spirit. We do not have to go find the Ark, worry about its loss or capture, or wait for it to arrive at the time of battle. The Ark is the indwelling blessing and power of the Holy Spirit within the core of our soul. The Ark is in our possession at all times. It is in our heart. It is the Father's intention to transform our heart into the same image and likeness of His own glorious heart. Do we perceive our marvelous inheritance?

The children of Israel relied on the Ark in order to enter the Promised Land of their inheritance in Canaan. Joshua instructed the priests of the tribe of Levi to carry the Ark of the Covenant into the flooded Jordan River. When their feet touched the surging water, the river was backed up in a heap.

> *Then the priests who bore the ark of the covenant of the LORD stood firm on dry ground in the midst of the Jordan; and all Israel crossed over on dry ground....*
> JOSHUA 3:17

This miraculous passage through the Jordan River was predicated on a priesthood who bore the Ark.

Now we are a royal priesthood through Spirit-birth. The Son has washed us from sin and made us to be kings and priests unto our God. As the heirs of God's Kingdom we have a promised land—a realm of profound inheritance—that awaits our possession. The only requirement is that of a priesthood who will hold up the Ark in the midst of unbelief so that all of God's people can fully possess their inheritance. We are to consider our calling in God to bear the ark so that all kindreds, tongues, tribes, peoples, and nations can cross over dry shod into the land of their promised heritage in Christ.

The Ark will again be exalted among the people to such a degree that the Earth will shake with the revelation of divine purpose. The reality of the Ark's presence, once known, will spread like wildfire. The old idolatry of the lost physical Ark will melt away as the people realize that the spiritual Ark is their personal heritage. The mad search for the lost artifact will cease when God's people experience the transition from the legalism and condemnation of the Old Covenant into the New Covenant of peace and righteousness.

The prophets of the Old Testament foretold the time when the physical Ark would no longer be important:

> *Then it shall come to pass, when you are multiplied and increased in the land in those days, says the LORD, that **they will say no more, "The ark of the covenant***

> ***of the Lord." It shall not come to mind, nor shall they remember it, nor shall they visit it, nor shall it be made anymore.*** JEREMIAH 3:16, EMPHASIS ADDED

Simply stated, we do not need a literal Ark located in a physical Tabernacle. That was just a pattern, and it was fulfilled two thousand years ago. The Son of God brought the good news that the true Ark dwells in Temples not made by hands. We possess this greatest of Temple treasures in our heart, where the resurrection life and power of the Son eternally springs forth as living water.

FROM THE GOLDEN ARK MY LORD DOES LEAD ME
INTO THE PROMISED LAND OF DIVINE DESTINY.

THE CHERUBIM

Key Words: Spirit Baptism

Significance

The cherubim signify baptism in the Holy Spirit. The believer, resting between the cherubim, receives the indwelling spiritual presence of the Father and Son. The Savior referred to this gift of the indwelling Spirit in various terms: the promise of the Father, the Spirit of truth, and the Comforter. Our baptism in the Holy Spirit seals the hope and promise of our inheritance in Christ.

Supportive Scriptures

> *Upon whom you see the Spirit descending, and remaining on Him, this is He* [the Son] *who baptizes with the Holy Spirit.* JOHN 1:33

> *"I* [John] *indeed baptized you with water, but He [the Son] will baptize you with the Holy Spirit." It came to pass in those days that Jesus came from Nazareth of Galilee, and was baptized by John in the Jordan. And immediately, coming up from the water, He saw the heavens parting and the Spirit descending upon Him like*

a dove. Then a voice came from heaven, "You are My beloved Son, in whom I am well pleased." MARK 1:8-11

"The Helper [Comforter], the Holy Spirit, whom the Father will send in My name, He will teach you all things, and bring to your remembrance all things that I said to you. JOHN 14:26

"...If I do not go away, the Helper [Comforter] will not come to you; but if I depart, I will send Him to you." JOHN 16:7

And by this we know that He [the Son] abides in us, by the Spirit whom He has given us. 1 JOHN 3:24

Physical Description

The cherubim emerged from the two ends of the Mercy Seat and overshadowed it with their majestic wings. The Aaronic priest, seeking guidance from God, would sit on the Mercy Seat beneath the outstretched wings of the cherubim. The fact that the cherubim were made of the same gold stock as the Mercy Seat, and that they overshadowed it, is a symbolic portrayal of the absolute interdependence of the crucifixion and the Resurrection. The pure gold of the Mercy Seat and cherubim indicates the righteousness of God: The priest sits on the gold and the gold surrounds him.

The mystery regarding the design of the cherubim, their size, their configuration, and their mystical beauty, directs our attention to the Spirit of God, its indescribable glory, and its indefinable virtue and power.

And you shall make two cherubim of gold; of hammered work you shall make them at the two ends of the mercy seat ... you shall make the cherubim at the two ends of it of one piece with the mercy seat. And the cherubim shall stretch out their wings above, covering the mercy seat with their wings, and they shall face one another; the faces of the cherubim shall be toward the mercy seat. EXODUS 25:18-20

We will shortly discover the profound meaning of these details: The cherubim and the Mercy Seat were of *one piece*, the cherubim faced one another, and the cherubim were mirror images of each other.

You shall put the mercy seat on top of the ark, and in the ark you shall put the Testimony that I will give you. ***And there I will meet with you, and I will speak with you from above the mercy seat, from between the two cherubim which are on the ark of the Testimony....*** EXODUS 25:21-22, EMPHASIS ADDED

In the Holy of Holies God established the Ark of the Covenant with its Mercy Seat overshadowed by the cherubim. There God would commune with man. This is the pattern God gave to Moses. Indeed, Moses experienced communion with the living God within the confines of the literal, physical Tabernacle in the wilderness over 3500 years ago, as follows:

Now when Moses went into the tabernacle of meeting to speak with Him, ***he heard the voice of One speaking to him*** *from above the mercy seat that was on the ark of the Testimony, from between the two cherubim;* ***thus He spoke to him.*** NUMBERS 7:89, EMPHASIS ADDED

This was an awesome historical precedent! The God of the universe would meet with man in a specially designed building according to God-appointed ritual and protocol. It is easy to understand why the Holy of Holies, and particularly the Ark of the Covenant, took on such reverent adulation among humanity even until this present time.

Spiritual Application

Under the Old Covenant of Law, access into the Holy of Holies was the exclusive domain of Moses, Aaron and his sons, and eventually the priests of the tribe of Levi. Under the Law very few men ever enjoyed the honor of sitting on the Mercy Seat beneath the golden wings of the cherubim. Few men, in fact, ever visited the inner hidden chamber of the Holy of Holies. The natural Tabernacle was extremely limited in the scope of its outreach and effect among the human family.

Conversely, the spiritual Temple introduced by the Savior offers unlimited outreach and universal effects. He inaugurated a Kingdom and Temple open unto all mankind by faith, rather than by religious works or by preeminent natural birthright. In our quest for truth we have come to the concept of the cherubim. Those who grasp the symbolic value of the cherubim will never be satisfied until they personally partake of this spiritual reality.

The cherubim symbolize the indwelling presence of the Father and Son. The cherubim are personally experienced as the baptism of the Holy Spirit—the coming of the Comforter to dwell in the human heart forever. The Holy Spirit—the cherubim—proceeded forth from the Father to baptize Jesus as He stood in the Jordan River. It was at this critical moment, when Jesus was baptized in both the water and the Spirit, that the Father made His eternal decree: "*This is My beloved Son, in whom I am well pleased*" (Matthew 3:17). The Son's Spirit baptism set the example for all the children of the Father. We must be born not only of water, but also of Spirit.

John the Baptist emphatically stated that Jesus would baptize the people of God with the Holy Spirit, as follows:

"*...this is He who baptizes with the Holy Spirit.*" JOHN 1:33

"...He will baptize you with the Holy Spirit." MARK 1:8

"...He will baptize you with the Holy Spirit and fire." MATTHEW 3:11

"...He will baptize you with the Holy Spirit and fire." LUKE 3:16

Jesus explained to His disciples that the Spirit would be given only after He was crucified and glorified. The disciples therefore believed in the promise of Spirit baptism, but they did not personally experience its fulfillment during the three-and-one-half years of the Savior's earthly ministry. The Holy Spirit—the Comforter—was present among the disciples as long as Jesus was physically present because He alone possessed the Spirit at that time. The disciples only knew the Spirit as they witnessed its manifestation in Jesus. Their hope was in the Son because He walked with the Father. Their security and comfort, confidence and strength, were in the Son. The Son, however, was not yet in them. He would have to physically depart from their midst before they could receive the same Spirit Comforter that dwelt in Him. Thus the crucifixion of the Son was not only essential for the remission of sin, but also as a necessary step in providing the believer with the gift of Spirit baptism.

Read prayerfully the teaching of the Son concerning Spirit baptism:

> *I will pray the Father, and He will give you another Helper* [Comforter], *that He may abide with you forever—the Spirit of truth, whom the world cannot receive, because it neither sees Him nor knows Him;* ***but you know Him, for He dwells with you and will be in you.*** *I will not leave you orphans* [comfortless]; *I will come to you. A little while longer and the world will see Me no more* [because of the crucifixion], ***but you*** [the

> believer] ***will see Me. Because I live, you will live also. At that day*** [the Day of Pentecost] ***you will know that I am in My Father, and you in Me, and I in you.*** John 14:16-20, emphasis added

The Savior stood among His disciples and proclaimed that the Comforter dwelt with them and that they knew Him. Indeed, the disciples knew their Master face-to-face, man-to-man. They honored and loved Him as their Comforter, and they were eyewitnesses of His majesty. But the Savior spoke beyond their present understanding when He told them that the Comforter would be in them, that they would see Him, and that they would live because the Son would live in them.

The disciples could not truly understand what He said until they experienced the Spirit baptism on the Day of Pentecost. "*These things I have spoken to you while being present with you*" (John 14:25). The Son knew of His impending death. As a wise and compassionate shepherd, He counseled His disciples on matters so very profound. The true unity of the Spirit awaited the disciples. They would grasp the meaning of the Savior's words only when the power of the Holy Spirit filled their Temples. The power of resurrection life would overwhelm them on the Day of Pentecost and they would experience the reality of His promise: "*I am in My Father, and you in Me, and I in you.*"

> "*The Helper [Comforter], the Holy Spirit, whom the Father will send in My name, He will teach you all things.* JOHN 14:26

All things spoken by the Savior to His disciples were later taught to them by the Spirit. His words in them became known as Spirit and life. The Spirit is referred to as "the Spirit of truth." The Spirit speaks truth always and never a lie. The Spirit is the pure expression of the truth such that one Scripture simply concludes: "*The Spirit is truth*" (1 John 5:6). The disciples were taught truth by the Spirit of truth, which dwelt in the Son, and later at Pentecost this same Spirit of truth made His abode in the hearts of the disciples. Both when He was physically present with them and later when He indwelt them by the Spirit, the disciples were taught the truth by the Truth.

The Spirit of truth that dwelt in the Son always testified of the Father. Consider the unbreakable bond between Father and Son. If we read carefully, we will discover this union between Father and Son as a pervasive, inviolate principle throughout the New Testament. The Spirit is variously referred to as the promise of the Father and the Spirit of the Son. It is one Holy Spirit, one holy life, known and experienced in fullness by both the Father and the Son. Some Scriptures state that Jesus baptizes people with the Spirit, while others state that the Spirit proceeds from the Father. This is not a contradiction, but instead is a beautiful affirmation that the very same life of the Father dwells in His Son. And, mystery of the ages, this same life of the Father is our inheritance in the Son.

This perfect unity of the Father and the Son is reflected in the cherubim. Consider the pattern that God revealed to Moses. There were two cherubim. They were made from one piece of gold stock. They were identical in size, shape, and configuration. They faced toward one another with their outstretched wings overshadowing the Mercy Seat. Moses, sitting on the Mercy Seat, could look above his head at the two cherubs and see that one looked just like the other. The Son made this revealing statement: "*He who has seen Me has seen the Father*" (John 14:9). And again He said: "*I and my Father are one*" (John 10:30). The Mercy Seat and the two cherubim were all of one piece. The Father made the firstborn Son to be His perfect reflection. The Son reveals the Father. They are two separate entities who abide in perfect unity. They are one in the divine nature, one in Spirit, one in truth, one in power, one in glory, and one in immortality.

The cherubim symbolize this unity between Father and Son. We become partakers of the very same unity of fellowship when we are baptized in the Spirit. We are dwelling upon the Mercy Seat between the cherubim when the Holy Spirit fills our Temple. We receive the Spirit—one Spirit—though it has several titles to indicate its multifaceted glory. It is the Spirit of the Son. It is the promise of the Father. It is the Spirit of truth. It is the Comforter. It is referred to as the Holy Spirit, the Spirit, the holy life, and the Holy Ghost. It yet remains one Spirit that testifies of the Father and Son. The two witnesses take up their abode in us when we truly dwell between the cherubim for the first time. Henceforth, we are possessors of the cherubim, having received the indwelling gift of the Holy Spirit.

> "*. . . We* [Father and Son] *will come unto him, and make our abode with him.*" JOHN 14:23, KJV

> "*That they all may be one, as You, Father, are in Me, and I in You; that they also may be one in Us, that the world may believe that You sent Me.*" JOHN 17:21

Jesus appeared to His disciples for forty days after His Resurrection. At the end of the forty days, He instructed them to wait together in Jerusalem in order to receive the cherubim experience. "*Behold, I send the Promise of My Father upon you; but tarry in the city of Jerusalem until you are endued with power from on high*" (Luke 24:49). Ten days would elapse from the time the Savior ascended into glory and the Day of Pentecost.

> "*John truly baptized with water, but you shall be baptized with the Holy Spirit not many days [ten days] from now.*" ACTS 1:5

> *While Peter was still speaking these words, the Holy Spirit fell upon all those who heard the word.... The gift of the Holy Spirit had been poured out on the Gentiles* [nations] *also. For they heard them speak with tongues and magnify God. Then Peter answered, "Can anyone forbid water, that these should not be baptized* ***who have received the Holy Spirit just as we have?"*** ACTS 10:44-47, EMPHASIS ADDED

Cornelius and those of his household were uncircumcised Gentiles. Peter was not allowed to fellowship with Gentiles under the Law of the Old Covenant. God used this situation to teach Peter, as well as the other apostles, that the gospel was for all nations. "*What God has cleansed you must not call common*" (Acts 10:15). The point pertinent to this discussion is that the gift of the Holy Spirit was poured out on the Gentiles—the nations—and was no longer the exclusive domain of a select few.

In this manner the good news spread from house to house, from city to city, and from nation to nation. Wherever the gospel was received there was an impartation of the gift of Spirit baptism. Peter said it quite plainly: "*God gave them the same gift as He gave us when we believed on the Lord Jesus Christ...* " (Acts 11:17). It was the same gift then, and it is the same gift today. It is our inheritance in the Anointed One. We are anointed by the same Spirit that raised Christ from the grave. We are heirs of the same power that filled the apostles at Pentecost. "*And by this* [Spirit baptism] *we know that He abides in us, by the Spirit which He has given us*" (1 John 3:24).

Sadly, many contemporary Christian assemblies teach against the Spirit baptism. They refute the gift of the Holy Spirit, which the Savior declared would be witnessed to the end of the Earth. To deny the free gift of Spirit baptism is to teach that the veil into the Holy of Holies was never torn asunder at the Savior's crucifixion. It is a carnal effort to close the door the Son has already opened for all people and for all times.

The same Spirit, which indwelt the Savior, His apostles, and all believers in the virgin Church, is readily available today. We have no less inheritance in God's Kingdom. As we declare this truth of Spirit baptism, we will witness its overwhelming power as God's people everywhere experience the cherubim.

The disciples already believed in the Savior when they experienced the cherubim on the Day of Pentecost. This is a critical insight deserving of prayerful consideration. From the perspective of the Temple treasures, the gate of faith was followed by the cherubim of the golden Ark. The disciples first received the gift of faith in the Son of God—the gate of the court. Then they received the gift of Spirit baptism—the cherubim of the Holy of Holies. In this way the entirety of all Temple treasures was sealed within their lives forever. Sealed first with the gift of faith, they were then sealed with the gift of Spirit baptism. This was the typical experience of all new believers.

Each disciple would be required to grow in grace and knowledge throughout their earthly sojourn. Each would experience fiery trials of their faith. Each would gain maturity and virtue as they developed into the divine nature. Yet each one was sealed by the Spirit when they first began their journey of growth and regeneration.

We should earnestly desire to be sealed by the Spirit just as our Savior was sealed. "*...because God the Father has set **His seal** on Him*" (John. 6:27, emphasis added). This special term, *seal*, means to stamp as with a signet or private mark for security and preservation. The Temple treasures are preserved in the Spirit. From the gate of the court to the Ark of the Holy of Holies, the treasures are sealed forever in the life of each believer. Not only do we receive the gift of faith, but also the gift of the cherubim. It is all a gift according to grace and not by works. We simply ask and then receive the free gift.

> *All the promises of God in Him are Yes, and in Him Amen, to the glory of God through us. Now He who*

> *establishes us with you in Christ and has anointed us is God,* ***who also has sealed us and given us the Spirit in our hearts as a guarantee.*** 2 CORINTHIANS 1:20-22, EMPHASIS ADDED

Every aspect of the court and Temple is a promise of God to each believer, and in God all these promised treasures are a resounding *Yes* and *Amen*! There is no doubt in Him, for in Him we have eternal security and the preservation of our souls. Notice it is *the glory of God through us*. And it is God who has anointed us. *Yes*, He has sealed our hearts with His own Spirit, and *Amen*, He has given us this unassailable guarantee.

This seal of God's Spirit is a personal guarantee from the eternal Father to each of His precious children. We should not underestimate its value. We must not allow the unbelief of many Christian leaders to cheat us from this special treasure.

> *In Him also we have obtained an inheritance.... In Him you also trusted, after you heard the word of truth, the gospel of your salvation;* ***in whom also, having believed*** [the gate of faith], ***you were sealed with the Holy Spirit of promise*** [the cherubim], ***who is the guarantee of our inheritance*** *until the redemption of the purchased possession, to the praise of His glory.* EPHESIANS 1:11, 13-14, EMPHASIS ADDED

It is to the glory of the Father and Son that we have been purchased through the work of the Cross and because of this we are the heirs of complete redemption from carnality and death in all their guises. Until the fullness of our redemption is made manifest, we are sealed with *the Spirit of promise* by which we know that every promise of the gospel of truth shall ultimately be manifested. Our inheritance in the Son is guaranteed by the indwelling presence of the Spirit.

There is a day of redemption within God's masterful plan of the ages, but also there is a day-to-day outworking of redemption in each believer's personal life. The *process* of redemption will eventually result in the *day* of redemption. There will come a day when the fullness of the Son is completely revealed in each of His people. A mature family of sons and daughters of God will show forth the Son's multifaceted wisdom and His immortal life. We are now the heirs of this eternal inheritance, but we must learn to walk in it. We learn through the leadership of the Spirit and the instruction of the truth to possess and eventually demonstrate all the promises of God in Christ. In the days of our processing and regeneration, we must take care to heed the indwelling Spirit of promise. *"Do not grieve the Holy Spirit of God, by whom you were* ***sealed*** *for the day of redemption"* (Ephesians 4:30, emphasis added).

We reiterate these critical points:

- The Savior received the gift of Spirit baptism when He was baptized in water by John.
- The 120 apostles and disciples received the gift of Spirit baptism on the Day of Pentecost.
- Every new believer was presented the same gift of Spirit baptism.
- The Word of God emphasizes that every believer—past, present, and future—is to be sealed by Spirit baptism unto their full inheritance.

The Apostle Paul asked a vital question that every believer should seriously consider:

> *"Did you receive the Holy Spirit when you believed?"*
> ACTS 19:2

Paul, along with the other apostles, would ask this question of those who already believed. You have believed unto salvation, you have been baptized in water, but have you received the cherubim? Have you been sealed by the Spirit? *"And when Paul had laid hands on them, the Holy Spirit came upon them, and they spoke with tongues and prophesied"* (Acts 19:6). It was Paul's earnest desire that God's people would realize the greatness of their inheritance in the Son.

Spirit baptism—the cherubim—is part of our inheritance in Christ. The word *Christ* means *the Anointing*. If we are "in Christ" we are in the Anointing of His Spirit. If Christ is in us as the hope of glory, then the anointing of Spirit baptism dwells within our Temple. If we are baptized into Jesus Christ, then we are filled to overflowing with His Spirit presence. God's grace invites each believer to enter the Holy of Holies to rest upon the Mercy Seat. Here, overshadowed by the spiritual presence of the Father and Son, the seeker is baptized in the Spirit.

Baptism means *to be overwhelmed,* or *completely covered.* To sit between the cherubim is to be overwhelmed by the power of the Holy Spirit, just as the disciples were overwhelmed on the Day of Pentecost. The human soul is filled by the Spirit, covered by the Spirit, indeed, overwhelmed by the Spirit. The soul is sealed, forever, with the Spirit of promise. This gift is ours because our Forerunner made the way into the Holy of Holies for us. He is our anchor within the veil both sure and steadfast.

The gift of the cherubim, once received, opens the way for further fellowship with the treasures found in the golden Ark. The firstborn Son established the Holy of Holies as our inheritance once and for all times. He guaranteed these Temple treasures as eternal promises sealed with His own Spirit.

CHERUBIM OF GLORY, DWELLING DEEP WITHIN,
FATHER AND SON ARE NOW MY NEAREST OF KIN.

THE MERCY SEAT

Key Word: Atonement

Significance

The Mercy Seat signifies the Savior's finished work of atonement by which we are reconciled to God. God's unlimited love, immeasurable grace, and boundless forgiveness are epitomized in the Mercy Seat. It is the secret dwelling place wherein we experience perfect unity with God.

Supportive Scriptures

He who dwells in the secret place of the Most High shall abide under the shadow of the Almighty. PSALM 91:1

For if when we were enemies we were reconciled to God through the death of His Son, much more, having been reconciled, we shall be saved by His life. And not only that, but we also rejoice in God through our Lord Jesus Christ, through whom we have now received the reconciliation. ROMANS 5:10-11

God, who is rich in mercy, because of His great love with which He loved us, even when we were dead in trespasses, made us alive together with Christ (by

> *grace you have been saved) and raised us up together, and made us sit together* [on the Mercy Seat] *in the heavenly places* [in the Holy of Holies] *in Christ Jesus.* EPHESIANS 2:4-6

> *Mercy triumphs over judgment.* JAMES 2:13

> *The Lord is very compassionate and merciful.* JAMES 5:11

> *Oh, satisfy us early with Your mercy, that we may rejoice and be glad all our days.* PSALM 90:14

> *Let us therefore come boldly to the throne of grace, that we may obtain mercy and find grace to help in time of need.* HEBREWS 4:16

Physical Description

The Mercy Seat, the lid of the golden Ark, was made of pure gold. It was three-and three-fourths feet in length and two-and-one-fourth feet in width. Its position on top of the Ark made it two-and-one-fourth feet off the ground. (See Exodus 25:10, 17.)

As previously mentioned, the cherubim and the Mercy Seat were made of one piece of gold stock. The Mercy Seat was never considered separately from its cherubim.

> *You* [Moses] *shall make a mercy seat of pure gold … And you shall make two cherubim of gold; of hammered work you shall make them at the two ends of the mercy seat.… You shall put the mercy seat on top of the ark, and in the ark you shall put the Testimony* [tables of stone] *that I will give you. And there I will meet with you, and I will speak with you from above the mercy seat. …* EXODUS 25:17-18, 21-22. (SEE ALSO EXODUS 37:6-9.)

Spiritual Application

The mercy of God radiates throughout the entire court and Temple. The Father manifested His infinite mercy through the gift of His Son. We discovered this when we first believed in the Son at the gate of faith. Mercy does not diminish as we progress into the Temple, but it always abounds and seems to increase beyond our ability to comprehend.

The Mercy Seat in the Holy of Holies epitomizes divine mercy. When we sit on the Mercy Seat between the cherubim, we are dwelling in the presence of the divine nature. We recognize the outstretched cherubim wings as the spiritual presence of the Father and Son, and we are overwhelmed by the realization that their divine presence has made its abode in our heart. The Mercy Seat positions us in direct fellowship with the living God. It is a spiritual realm in which the soul is flooded with the reality of the atonement.

The atonement is not a difficult concept if we consider it in terms of unity, oneness, and perfect harmony. To experience the Mercy Seat is deeper than intellectual thought, for it involves the totality of our identity as a vessel known of God from the foundation of the world. We are reunited—eternally reconciled—with our heavenly Father through the indwelling life of His Son. He that has the Son has life. God has given us eternal life and this life is in His Son.

Mercy Seat is an ancient term. It has been translated into English as *atonement*, *propitiation*, and *lid of the Ark*. These three terms direct our attention to the Savior's death on the Cross and His Resurrection from the grave. We are reconciled to God through the death of His Son and we are saved by His resurrection life.

The Old Covenant of Law was structured in such a way that the Israelites continually appeased God through outward, physical offerings and sacrifices. These external offerings and sacrifices were done for the sake of atonement. For over fifteen hundred years, it was clearly demonstrated that these natural works of atonement did not produce reconciliation between man and his God. Efforts at atonement under the Law did not and could not create the divine nature within the human heart. The blood of bulls and goats and all manner of animal sacrifices failed to bring man into perfect unity (at-one-ment) with God.

The term *atonement* is used only once in the King James Version of the New Testament, as follows:

> *We also joy in God through our Lord Jesus Christ, by whom we have now received the* ***atonement****.* ROMANS 5:11, KJV, EMPHASIS ADDED

Make a strong mental note of this key phrase: *We have now received the atonement*. It is not something we are looking to receive. Nor is it something for which we must work, labor, and struggle to achieve. It is done! The atonement was achieved, accomplished, and fulfilled at the Cross and is God's free gift for humanity for all times and places.

Most Bible translations render the word *atonement* as reconciliation. In the following verses the word for atonement has been translated as *reconciled, reconciling*, and *reconciliation*. These verses sum up the facts concerning our atonement in Christ:

> *Now all things are of God, who has* ***reconciled*** *us to Himself through Jesus Christ, and has given us the ministry of* ***reconciliation****, that is, that God was in Christ* ***reconciling*** *the world to Himself, not imputing their trespasses to them, and has committed to us the word of* ***reconciliation****. Now then, we are ambassadors for Christ, as though God were pleading through us: we implore you on Christ's behalf, be* ***reconciled*** *to God. For He made Him who knew no sin to be sin for us, that we might become the righteousness of God in Him.* 2 CORINTHIANS 5:18-21, EMPHASIS ADDED

Just prior to His last breath as He hung on the Cross, the Savior uttered three profound words: *"It is finished!"* (John 19:30). He was aware of the Old Testament Scriptures that consistently pointed to the need of atonement, or reconciliation, between God and man. He realized that the daily ritual of animal sacrifices under the Law foreshadowed His death on the Cross. He recognized Himself as the Passover Lamb who atones for the sins of the people. He knew He was chosen to be the Lamb slain from the foundation of the world. This was His calling, and He fulfilled the purpose of the Cross in complete obedience to the will of His Father. Based upon the Son's declaration that *"It is finished,"* we have inherited the right to declare the truth written by Paul: *We have now received the atonement.*

We have received the Mercy Seat, the atonement, because we have been reconciled to God. As we behold the mercy of God that is represented by the Mercy Seat, we are able to see into His great heart of love for the human family. His intentions toward humanity are based upon mercy, not condemnation. His motivation is divine love, not wrath. Keep in mind that the golden Mercy Seat covers the golden Ark and is overshadowed by the golden cherubim. The righteousness of God abounds in our lives when we embrace the mercy extended to us through His Son. Thus, the Mercy Seat is charged with meaning in relationship to the New Covenant of grace and truth. It is an evocative portrayal of the Father's primary motivation: mercy and love.

Propitiation is another key term used in place of Mercy Seat. Propitiation simply means that our reconciliation to God is an accomplished fact. Mercy has been granted and endures triumphantly. The following Scriptures provide insight into the propitiation, which has been freely bestowed on mankind through faith in the Son.

> *Being justified freely by His grace through the redemption that is in Christ Jesus, whom God set forth*

as a propitiation [atonement] *by His blood, through faith, to demonstrate His righteousness, because in His forbearance God had passed over the sins that were previously committed.* ROMANS 3:24-25

Therefore, in all things He had to be made like His brethren, that He might be a merciful and faithful High Priest in things pertaining to God, to make propitiation [atonement] *for the sins of the people.* HEBREWS 2:17

And He Himself is the propitiation [atonement] *for our sins, and not for ours only but also for the whole world.* 1 JOHN 2:2

In this is love, not that we loved God, but that He loved us and sent His Son to be the propitiation [atonement] *for our sins.* 1 JOHN 4:10

Love was the motivation of the Father in sending His Son to die for sin. Mercy was the essential element of the Father's character, and He instilled this merciful nature in His firstborn Son. It was the Father's heart before the foundation of the Earth to produce a vast family of sons and daughters who would be made partakers of His divine nature. They would be transformed into the image and likeness of the firstborn—a merciful and faithful High Priest. To accomplish the predestined purpose of the plan of the ages, the Father sent the Son as a gift to every human soul. He desires that all shall know the Son as the propitiation—the atonement—the reconciliation, indeed, the Mercy Seat. The Father graciously invites His children to rest on the Mercy Seat in the Holy of Holies of the Temple, which we are in Him.

It is because of the forgiveness and reconciliation found at the Mercy Seat that we can have fellowship with the Father and Son. Truly our fellowship is with the Father and Son as we enter into their spiritual presence. It is the Spirit that quickens. The same Holy Spirit who led Jesus in His earthly ministry to its completion on the Cross, is the same Spirit that raised Him from the grave. It is this same Spirit that is now a treasure in our earthen vessels. For we know that we are the Temple of God and His Spirit dwells within. He has sent the Spirit of His Son into our hearts. Nothing could convey with more purity the infinite mercy of our God.

Listen to the voice of mercy:

> *I will send you another Comforter. When He, the Spirit of truth, is come, He will guide you into all Truth. I will be their God and they shall be My people. I will walk in them and talk in them. I will write My law in their hearts.*

These promises of God find powerful expression in the Mercy Seat. The Lord told Moses: "*I will appear* [to you] *in the cloud above the mercy seat*" (Leviticus 16:2). This promise was fulfilled: "*Moses ... heard the voice of One speaking to him from above the mercy seat*" (Numbers 7:89).

Moses, direct recipient of the Tabernacle pattern, recognized the Mercy Seat as the place wherein God communes with man. God instructed Moses in clear terms: "*You shall put the mercy seat on top of the ark.... **And there I will meet with you, and I will speak with you from above the mercy seat...***" (Exodus 25:21-22, emphasis added). Moses understood these instructions in a literal sense in regard to the physical Ark located in the temporal Tabernacle in the wilderness. It was Moses' understanding that he had to literally sit on the actual Mercy Seat in order to commune with God. To Moses the Tabernacle was of physical substance and every aspect of it was governed by carefully prescribed formalities and rituals. Most of the rituals involved the blood of animals—an endless ritualistic cycle of atoning exercises. Moses set the pattern for the Aaronic priesthood to follow. They diligently repeated the pattern for centuries.

The love and mercy of God appeared when He sent His Son to be the Savior of the world. The Son fulfilled the pattern in a short three-and-one-half-year timeframe through the crucifixion and Resurrection. He exceedingly transcended the Old Covenant. In doing so He provided a new and living way. Our study of the pattern yields much wisdom. We are especially impressed by the sharp contrast between the Old Testament of Law and the New Testament of grace and truth. Our inheritance in the Son makes us to be heirs of a far greater Covenant with far greater promises! No longer must we practice timeworn formalities and rigid rituals in order to enter Holy Places made by human hands. Instead we enter into the presence of the Spirit, rejoice in Christ Jesus, have no confidence in the flesh, and in the Spirit we are graciously invited to enter the Holy of Holies to rest upon the Mercy Seat. Here, in full realization of the atonement, God meets with us and even speaks in us as we give all due diligence and honor to Him.

> *Not by works of righteousness which we have done, but according to His mercy He saved us, through the washing of regeneration and renewing of the Holy Spirit.* TITUS 3:5

It is well understood that we do not approach the Holy of Holies through our own works of righteousness. We enter the inner veil because we know it was torn in two at the crucifixion of the Savior. We rest upon the Mercy Seat because we know the Savior fulfilled the atonement through His death on the Cross. We dwell between the cherubim to receive the gift of Spirit baptism because it is the promise of the Father granted through His Son.

The washing of regeneration begins in the court at the gate of faith. Our direct personal participation with the vessels of the court and the Temple washes us from every carnal hindrance in the ongoing process of regeneration. However, there is an ultimate realization of the Son's sacrificial blood, which is known only in the Holy of Holies upon the Mercy Seat. It was according to His mercy that He saved us. The Mercy Seat is known among those who have come through great tribulation and have washed their robes (character) white in the blood of the Lamb.

The renewing of the Holy Spirit also begins in the court at the gate of faith. Once again, however, it is only imparted as a gift into our own heart when we enter the Holy of Holies to rest on the Mercy Seat. The spiritual presence of the Father and Son, the cherubim, make their abode in our Temple. Henceforth, the Holy Spirit is continually renewed throughout our earthly sojourn as we learn to yield to the leadership of the Spirit. The gift of the Holy Spirit is renewed in the human soul like a river of living water that never runs dry.

Truly the new day dawns when we rest upon the Mercy Seat. We are now joined with all believers around the globe to offer heartfelt worship to our merciful Father "*...who* ***according to His abundant mercy*** *has begotten us again to a living hope through the resurrection of Jesus Christ from the dead*" (1 Peter 1:3, emphasis added).

MERCY SEAT: INNER REALM OF INFINITE REST.
IN THE RIGHTEOUSNESS OF THE SON I AM BLESSED.

THE TWO TABLETS OF STONE

Key Words: Divine Nature

Significance

The Ten Commandments, written on two tablets of stone by the finger of God, signify the revelation of the human heart. Each Commandment identifies a specific trait of the human nature that is overcome by the divine nature of pure love. Love fulfills the Law.

Supportive Scriptures

The law of the Spirit of life in Christ Jesus has made me free from the law of sin and death. ROMANS 8:2

Christ has redeemed us from the curse of the law, having become a curse for us.... GALATIANS 3:13

All the law is fulfilled in one word, even in this: "You shall love your neighbor as yourself." GALATIANS 5:14

"...You shall love the Lord your God with all your heart, with all your soul, and with all your mind. This is the first and great commandment. And the second is like it:

You shall love your neighbor as yourself. On these two commandments hang all the Law and the Prophets." MATTHEW 22:37-40

This is the covenant that I will make … I will put My laws in their mind and write them on their hearts; and I will be their God, and they shall be My people.… All shall know Me, from the least of them to the greatest of them. For I will be merciful to their unrighteousness, and their sins and their lawless deeds I will remember no more. HEBREWS 8:10-12

Physical Description

God inscribed the Ten Commandments in two stone tablets.

And Moses turned and went down from the mountain, and the two tablets of the Testimony were in his hand. The tablets were written on both sides; on the one side and on the other they were written. Now the tablets were the work of God, and the writing was the writing of God engraved on the tablets. EXODUS 32:15-16

The actual dimensions of the stone tablets are not provided. The important point is that God wrote His Commandments in stone and gave the tablets to Moses with instructions to place them in the Ark of the Covenant. *"Then I* [Moses] *turned and came down from the mountain, and* ***put the tablets in the ark*** *which I had made; and there they are, just as the LORD commanded me"* (Deuteronomy 10:5, emphasis added). (See also Exodus 40:20.)

The two stone tablets are consistently referred to as *the Testimony*. (See Exodus 25:16, 21, 22; 26:33; 30:26; 40:21.) Therefore the golden Ark was called the Ark of Testimony because it contained the stone tablets. In addition, the two stone tablets are referenced as *the tablets of the covenant* (see Deuteronomy 9:11) because the central issue of the Old Covenant, or Testament, was the law of sin governing the human heart. The prophets and apostles made numerous references to the stone tablets as the Law, the Ten Commandments, and the tablets of the Covenant. Paul makes note of the two stone tablets in Hebrews 9:4: "*...the ark of the covenant overlaid on all sides with gold, in which were the golden pot that had the manna, Aaron's rod that budded, and the* ***tablets of the covenant***" (emphasis added).

Spiritual Application

God inscribed the Ten Commandments into stone tablets not once, but twice. This dramatic historic episode yields much understanding if we have the courage to examine it closely.

Moses, the man chosen by God to receive the Law, broke the original set of tablets in a fit of anger because the people of Israel had fallen into idolatry. They worshiped a golden calf in carnal revelry and crass celebration during the time that Moses was on Mount Sinai with God. The Israelites realized that Moses had led them out of Egyptian bondage through the direct intervention of God's hand. They also knew that Moses was called by the voice of God to meet with Him on the mount. They witnessed the visible signs of God's majesty that covered the mount—the fire, the smoke, the quaking, and the sound of trumpets. In spite of this profound awareness that Moses was chosen of God and that He was on the mount meeting with God, the people blatantly dishonored both Moses and God.

In their disobedience the Israelites defiled the Law at the very same hour in which it was being inscribed in stone by the finger of God. They idolized a golden calf rather than worship God. They spoke lies and bore false witness. They committed fornication and adultery. They were a rebellious and stiff-necked people. It was a sad and despicable display of human nature. Why did it happen? Simply put, the people did not have the Law of God written in their hearts. It demonstrated the vast gulf between the Law written on stone tablets versus the law of sin written in the hearts of the people.

As a matter of fact, the Covenant of Law never did deliver the people from the bondage of human nature. Throughout the timeframe of the Law Covenant—over fifteen hundred years—a key principle was forever established: An external code of written Law can affect the outer man, but it can never change the human heart. God provided this stark picture of the human nature among the Israelites so that all following generations could study it and learn. His chosen people yielded themselves to the law of sin at the very time when He was revealing the Ten Commandments. This was not a coincidence. It was an open portrayal of the law of sin and death governing the unregenerate heart of mankind.

Moses was so disturbed by this rank display of the self-nature that He broke the stone tablets that contained the Ten Commandments. God gave the Law, but it was broken by His chosen people as they gave themselves to the passions of the human nature, and it was literally broken by Moses as he shattered the stone tablets upon the ground. This lesson was given at the very inception of the Law Covenant and was then expounded upon for fifteen centuries until the appearance of the Savior. It is a lesson that implies that the Law was made to be broken because the human heart is not transformed by Law. Deliverance does not come by Law but only by the new birth through faith in the Son of God.

It is God's intention that we understand the law of sin and death. He had Moses place the Ten Commandments in the golden Ark as an emphatic declaration that we are to not only understand the human nature, but indeed we are to be made free from its carnal dominion. The tablets of stone were called the Testimony because they testify of the condition of the human heart. The innate carnality of the human heart is accurately assessed by the words of the prophet: "*The heart is deceitful above all things, and desperately wicked; who can know it*? (Jeremiah 17:9).

The self-nature within our own heart is the silent assassin and we must understand its pervasive and subtle influence. Paul the apostle recognized the law of sin and death within his own nature. Even though Paul was a believer and an apostle, yet he cried out to God on behalf of all God's people: "*O wretched man that I am! Who will deliver me from this body of death? I thank God—through Jesus Christ our Lord! So then, with the mind I myself serve the law of God, but with the flesh* [the heart] *the law of sin*" (Romans 7:24-25). Paul had become aware that his mind, disciplined and dedicated to truth, was challenged and indeed undermined by the law of sin in his own heart.

Paul identified two laws that dwell in our human Temples. One law, born in us through natural birth and nurtured by a carnal world, is the innate law of sin and death. The other law, received through our new birth in Christ and nurtured by the Spirit and Word, is the law of God. The law of sin and death is overcome as we learn to walk in the Spirit and Word of the Lord. In its most pristine expression, the law of God is His divine nature of pure love. God's nature of pure love is referred to as the perfect law of liberty because the divine nature automatically fulfills the Ten Commandments. It is our earnest desire to be partakers of this perfect law—the divine nature. Yet it is God's expectation that we, as mature sons and daughters, will come to understand the role of the Ten Commandments written and engraved on two tablets of stone.

Two implies witnesses. Two tablets of stone present two witnesses that testify to the law of sin that rules the human nature. It is this Testimony that was placed in the Ark within the Holy of Holies. Paul acknowledged this Testimony throughout his epistles as he carefully explained the fact that the Law does not bring deliverance. The Old Covenant was based on Law. The New Covenant was based on the transforming life of the Son of God. "*The law made nothing perfect; on the other hand, there is the bringing in of a better hope, through which we draw near to God"* (Hebrews 7:19). The Law bluntly and irrevocably declared that all humans are bound by their own inner sin nature.

Sin means to miss the mark. The firstborn Son is the mark, or image, to which we aspire, but the Testimony of the stone tablets insists that we can never attain the mark. The tablets make the incessant point that we must ever strive to keep the Law. It is written in stone that we stand accursed and condemned as carnal creatures subject to the bondage of corruption forever. The Law was written on both sides of the stone tablets to show that we cannot escape its condemnation; that no matter how we approach the Law it will declare our bondage to sin. The Law states the case of the human nature: It is subject to vanity and corruption. God wants His people to understand the Law and its relationship to the human nature. Once we gain this understanding, we can proclaim the victory like our brother Paul: Thanks be unto God—He sent His Son to provide the way of salvation and complete deliverance.

The revelation of the Son brings us to this hopeful conclusion: *"The law of the Spirit of life in Christ Jesus has made me free from the law of sin and death"* (Romans 8:2). The law of the Spirit transcends the law of sin and death. The dominion of God's Kingdom overwhelms the dominion of carnality. Light dispels darkness. The divine nature supplants the human nature. We joyfully bear the mark of the high calling when we walk in the anointing of the Spirit. The mark of a mature son or daughter of God emerges as we are changed into the image of the Son. The golden covering of the Ark is established in our hearts through the infusion of God's own righteousness.

The Testimony of the golden Ark in Christ—in the anointing of His Spirit—is far different from the testimony of the fallen human nature under the condemnation of the literal Law. *"By the law is the knowledge of sin"* (Romans 3:20). The Testimony engraved on stone tablets brought the knowledge of sin into stark clarity. That is to say, the Ten Commandments identified every human heart as a prisoner of ten carnal traits. It identified the law of sin within our own human nature, which was inclined to do what each of the Commandments said not to do. Paul wrote that when he desired to do good, evil was yet present. He pointed to an inner nature, a hidden source of carnality, which he termed *the law* of sin and death. We must recognize the absolute need for a new divine nature, a new source of life, indeed, a new law of the Spirit. "*Walk in the Spirit and you shall not fulfill the lust of the flesh*" (Galatians 5:16) and "*As many as are led by the Spirit of God, these are sons of God*" (Romans 8:14).

Christians are commonly taught that the primary goal is to keep the Ten Commandments. They are able to fulfill this goal in outward behavior with varying degrees of success depending upon their self-will and discipline. But this is not the same as being made free from sin through the power of the indwelling Christ. The Law works wrath. By the Law is the knowledge of sin. The New Covenant teaches that the Law was only a schoolmaster to bring us to Christ. Many who have been in bondage to the Law will rejoice to learn that the Law of Ten Commandments—written in stone—is called *the ministry of death*.

> ***If the ministry of death, written and engraved on stones,*** *was glorious, so that the children of Israel could not look steadily at the face of Moses because of the glory of his countenance, which glory was passing away,* ***how will the ministry of the Spirit not be more glorious?***
> 2 CORINTHIANS 3:7-8, EMPHASIS ADDED

The Covenant of Law—based on the Testimony of the Ten Commandments—possessed a certain degree of glory because it provided the knowledge of sin. However, it was God's intent that this glory of the Law would pass away in the light of the more glorious New Covenant founded in the Son.

Many good Christians, frustrated in the struggle to combine the Law of the Old Testament with the grace and truth of the New Testament, will be pleasantly surprised to realize that the Law was called *the ministry of condemnation.*

> *If* ***the ministry of condemnation*** *had glory, the ministry of righteousness exceeds much more in glory.*
> 2 CORINTHIANS 3:9, EMPHASIS ADDED

The written code of Law is a ministry of condemnation: It establishes sin but it never brings freedom from sin. Freedom from sin only comes through the ministry of righteousness. God's righteousness takes dominion in our heart through the presence of His Spirit and Word. The new man of the Spirit is birthed within. The principles of God's Word are written into our character by the Spirit. The darkness of carnality is vanquished when the light of the Word of God takes up its abode in our heart. "*For God, who commanded the light to shine out of darkness, hath shined in our hearts, to give the light of the knowledge of the glory of God in the face of Jesus Christ*" (2 Corinthians 4:6, KJV).

We receive the golden treasures of righteousness as a gift of faith. We embrace the golden inheritance that God has promised. We embrace the gold of the cherubim, the gold of the Mercy Seat, and the gold of the golden Ark. All of this golden inheritance we embrace as a new nature which fulfills the Law. We embrace this heritage in the Spirit because we realize that the Spirit alone can engraft the Word into the fleshly tablets of our heart.

> *You are our epistle written in our hearts, known and read by all men; clearly you are an epistle of Christ, ministered by us,* ***written not with ink but by the Spirit of the living***

> ***God, not on tablets of stone but on tablets of flesh, that is, of the heart.*** 2 CORINTHIANS 3:2-3, EMPHASIS ADDED

The new birth, which we experience through faith in the Son of God, culminates in the divine nature. We grow and grow until we are totally one with Him. Tablets of stone are transformed into fleshly tablets of the heart, openly declaring the law of the Spirit of life. Jesus Christ was not sent as a gift from the Father so that we would spend our existence struggling to keep the written code of Law. The gift of the Son established the law of the Spirit of life. If the Law of the Old Testament was the ultimate answer, then there was no need for the New Testament of grace and truth. Grace and truth fulfill the Law by the birthing of resurrection life within our very heart—in the solar plexus of our being—in the golden Ark. Here, hidden deep within as a treasure in an earthen vessel, eternal life springs forth.

The great sweeping power of resurrection life will birth a new day when we take hold of these profound principles:

> *Therefore, my brethren, you also have become dead to the law through the body of Christ.* ROMANS 7:4

> *Christ is the end of the law for righteousness to everyone who believes.* ROMANS 10:4

> *Christ has redeemed us from the curse of the law, having become a curse for us.* GALATIANS 3:13

> *All the law is fulfilled in one word, even in this: "You shall love your neighbor as yourself."* GALATIANS 5:14

The Spirit of God writes His law of divine love into our hearts. Once a believer has been overwhelmed—baptized—in the love of God, then they know the difference between the Old Covenant founded on Law and the New Covenant founded on the Spirit and Word of the Son of God. It is a vast difference and a marvelous realization. Love fulfills the Law. Truly, this is the simplicity found only in Christ, the Anointed One.

The Anointed One told us what we should do: We shall love the Lord completely and we shall love our neighbor as our self. On these two commandments hang all the Law and the Prophets. (See Matthew 22:37-40.) Jesus condensed the Old Testament down to these two awesome principles that establish divine love as the primary goal. He taught that the entire Old Testament—all the noble words written in the Law and the Prophets—was dependent for its fulfillment upon divine love. Love God. Love humanity. The manifestation of these two principles of love fulfills the two stone tablets of Law.

> *Love does no harm to a neighbor; therefore love is the fulfillment of the law.* ROMANS 13:10

The love of God, the essence of His divine nature, surpasses the realm of normal human experience. His love is known by the Holy Spirit who dwells in the hearts of His people. This is cause for much gladness and joy. The two tablets of stone no longer testify against us. Instead they yield up the life-giving Testimony that God's love dwells in man. "*We have known and believed the love that God has for us. God is love, and he who abides in love abides in God, and God in him*" (1 John 4:16). Herein are the stone tablets fulfilled.

TESTIMONY OF THE ARK, NO MORE IN STONE:
IT SPEAKS FROM THE HEART, GOD'S LOVE MADE KNOWN.

THE HIDDEN MANNA

Key Word: Revelation

Significance

The hidden manna signifies the revelation of truth. Here, in the living presence of the Father and Son, the mysteries of the Kingdom of Heaven are made known. The golden pot of manna in the Ark of the Covenant is God's assurance of an eternal provision for every need.

Supportive Scriptures

He who has an ear, let him hear what the Spirit says to the churches. To him who overcomes I will give some of the hidden manna to eat. REVELATION 2:17

"This is the bread which came down from heaven—not as your fathers ate the manna, and are dead. He who eats this bread will live forever." JOHN 6:58

"It has been given to you to know the mysteries of the kingdom of heaven...." MATTHEW 13:11

We... ask that you may be filled with the knowledge of His will in all wisdom and spiritual understanding. COLOSSIANS 1:9

"There is a God in heaven who reveals secrets." DANIEL 2:28

Physical Description

God provided manna from Heaven to feed the Israelites for forty years. (See Exodus 16:35.) The manna was not easily defined even in Moses' day. The word *manna* means, "What is it?" This was the expression used by the people of Israel when they first found the God-given manna lying upon the ground. The Scriptures provide some details as to the nature of manna.

And when the layer of dew lifted, there, on the surface of the wilderness, was a small round substance, as fine as frost on the ground. So when the children of Israel saw it, they said to one another, "What is it?" For they did not know what it was. And Moses said to them, "This is the bread which the LORD *has given you to eat."* EXODUS 16:14-15

And it was like white coriander seed, and the taste of it was like wafers made with honey. EXODUS 16:31

The people went about and gathered it, ground it on millstones or beat it in the mortar, cooked it in pans, and made cakes of it; and its taste was like the taste of pastry prepared with oil. NUMBERS 11:8

Take note that the manna was provided in a miraculous manner for the benefit of the people, yet they still had to gather it, grind it, and make edible cakes of it.

The manna was to be gathered in the morning each day of the week except on the Sabbath. The people were limited in the amount they could gather—"*...one omer for each person*" (Exodus 16:16). An *omer* was approximately equivalent to three-tenths of an English peck, or six-and-one-half pints. On the sixth day of the week, however, they were to gather "*...twice as much bread, two omers for each one*" (Exodus 16: 22). The double portion provided for the Sabbath.

The Lord commanded Moses to put one omer of manna in a pot "*...to be kept for your generations, that they may see the bread with which I fed you in the wilderness, when I brought you out of the land of Egypt*" (Exodus 16:32). This golden pot of manna was placed by Aaron "*...before the Testimony, to be kept*" (Exodus 16:34). The Testimony, of course, referred to the two stone tablets in the Ark of the Covenant. Paul makes note of the golden pot of manna in Hebrews 9:4: "*...the ark of the covenant overlaid on all sides with gold, in which were the golden pot that had the manna, Aaron's rod that budded, and the tablets of the covenant.*"

Spiritual Application

We have to be impressed by the miraculous quality of the manna. It appeared on the ground every morning, six days per week, for forty years. The Israelites would gather it early in the morning, for the heat of the sun caused the manna to quickly melt away. If anyone tried to gather more than an omer per day in order to store up an extra supply, it would breed worms and stink. Yet when they obeyed God by gathering up a double portion for the Sabbath, the manna retained its integrity for an extra day. Impressively, the manna kept the Israelites healthy throughout their forty years in the wilderness.

Also consider that the golden pot with its omer of manna was miraculously preserved within the Ark for many generations. This same miraculous quality is to be ascribed to the hidden manna. It is an infinite source of divine revelation. It is the impartation of divine understanding from an omniscient God to each faithful seeker.

We must expand our concepts beyond the literal golden pot of manna hid away in the physical Ark. The literal manna fed the children of Israel and kept them healthy for a full generation in the wilderness. Far greater is the spiritual manna that can feed the family of God throughout all generations. The source of the hidden manna is never exhausted because there is no end to God's wisdom. "*...His understanding is infinite*" (Psalm 147:5). It is universally available to all mankind, and yet it is revealed discreetly and wisely to each individual by the Spirit as they progress into their Temple treasures.

God instructed Moses to keep a sample of the manna in the Ark so that future generations would understand the miraculous manner in which God provided for His people. There was never a lack of manna during the forty years. Every individual and family had plenty of Heaven-sent bread to eat. This historic event in which God nourished His people through divine intervention is our spiritual example. Our Father will supply spiritual revelation of divine wisdom that is more than sufficient. He will supply the more magnificent manna promised by our Savior.

> "*I am the bread of life. Your fathers ate the manna in the wilderness, and are dead.... I am the living bread which came down from heaven. If anyone eats of this bread, he will live forever; and the bread that I shall give is My flesh, which I shall give for the life of the world.... As the living Father sent Me, and I live because of the Father, so he who feeds on Me will live because of Me.*"
> JOHN 6:48-49, 51, 57

The analogy with bread implies a food source, or a means of sustenance. The Savior utilizes the historic context of manna in the wilderness to introduce the higher concept of *living bread.* He is the living bread that came down from Heaven. The spiritual manna, revealed from Heaven, is far greater than the literal manna that fed the natural man. The living bread is the Son of God, and His life has the capacity to feed, nourish, and sustain the human soul throughout eternity.

Jesus said, *"I am the living bread which came down from heaven."* It is helpful to visualize Heaven as the golden Ark in the Holy of Holies. The living bread, the hidden manna—Jesus Christ—revealed himself unto mankind. He made the living bread available by placing it on the showbread table. Therefore the showbread in the Holy Place is a direct result of the hidden manna in the Holy of Holies. The Son (hidden manna) taught truth (showbread) to His twelve apostles. He gave them the bread from Heaven. When the apostles spoke and wrote this truth (bread), it became the twelve loaves of unleavened bread on the showbread table.

The apostles recognized and honored Jesus as the living bread because this was revealed to them by the Spirit. They received the bread by spiritual revelation. They spoke and wrote the bread by the inspiration of the Spirit. This is our example. We partake of the showbread in the light of the spiritual inspiration from the candlestick. There is no other source of light in the Holy Place except the candlestick. It means we partake of the showbread as we dwell in the Spirit of God. The showbread was given by revelation of the Spirit, and that is the only way we can receive it.

The showbread is readily available for study in the New Testament. We are blessed when we open our Bibles to read the truth that came from Heaven. We can read in the light of spiritual understanding that comes from the candlestick. However, every seeker encounters certain portions of truth doctrine (showbread) that are difficult to grasp. Often the showbread causes the seeker to think deeply and to ask profound questions.

The candlestick, with its sevenfold expression of the Spirit, does indeed illuminate our understanding of the showbread. And yet it is encouraging to realize that the knowledge of truth gained from the showbread can be supplemented by the hidden manna. The hidden manna backs up the showbread with unlimited supplies of spiritual revelation. In fact, the knowledge contained in the twelve loaves of showbread finds its source in the hidden manna. All showbread originates as hidden manna. In this pattern for the Temple, God wants His people to have confidence that their food supply will never run out. He provides showbread as a constant foundational supply, but He also provides the golden pot of hidden manna as a source of living bread that cannot be exhausted. God wants His people to know it is possible to enter the Holy of Holies in order to receive direct revelation concerning profound questions of doctrine.

In addition to its ability to add revelatory understanding to the truth doctrine, the hidden manna can also provide guidance to the challenges and dilemmas presented by these modern times. Our contemporary world with its global economy and ultra technology presents complex issues that can only be answered by divine wisdom. The golden pot of hidden manna is our God-given assurance that He will make every essential spiritual provision. The time will come when we will have national leadership who are mature in God's Temple. Leaders who are burdened with heavy responsibility will learn to approach the throne of grace to seek God's guidance. They will realize the hidden manna is available to those who walk with God in the Temple.

The Israelites left their tents early each morning in order to gather their daily supply of manna. They were diligent in this daily gathering of manna because they were hungry. Their hunger was met by divine provision, but they had to desire the manna enough to go gather it up. In a similar way, the Son of God has established the hidden manna such that there is no shortage of divine provision. However, the people of God have to be hungry enough to seek out the revelation of truth thatHe has made available. Once the daily manna was gathered, the Israelites had to process it into edible bread. The manna had to be ground very fine and then cooked. These details imply a certain amount of processing is needed. Indeed, we must have a hunger for righteousness. We must seek wisdom from above. We must be willing to ask questions, to ponder, to meditate, and to pray.

It has always been God's intention to reveal the mysteries of His Kingdom to His people. His intention is validated by the golden pot of hidden manna. Its placement beneath the Mercy Seat within the Ark is symbolic of divine provision. This provision of hidden manna is as certain as our faith in the Savior, for He opened the way into the Holy of Holies. He also provided open access to the Mercy Seat through His atoning sacrifice upon the Cross. Again, He sent the Spirit baptism, exemplified by the cherubim, whose extended golden wings welcome each seeker.

The contents of the golden Ark—tablets of stone, hidden manna, and Aaron's rod—are integral components of our inheritance in Christ. Our heavenly Father sent His Son so that we would know the truth concerning spiritual mysteries hidden since the foundation of the world. The following statement by the Savior, spoken to His disciples, applies just as well to us today:

> *"It has been given to you to know the mysteries of the kingdom of heaven...."* MATTHEW 13:11

Mysteries mean secrets. The Son of God taught secrets, or hidden manna, which revealed the Kingdom of Heaven to the apostles. It was this revelation of the knowledge of truth that established the New Covenant in Word—divine principles of truth. The apostles made the bread of Heaven available on the showbread table in the form of written Scriptures. Truth from the Son became the truth doctrine, or showbread, such that all following generations would have access to the bread that came from Heaven. The revelation of truth received by the apostles is now our revelation in Christ, in the Spirit—yes, indeed, in the anointing of the Son. The mysteries of the kingdom are the heritage of God's people today, and in every age, because the Spirit and truth of the Son are incorruptible, immutable, and immortal.

It is not enough just to read principles of truth in the Bible, or to hear them spoken. Truth must be revealed by the Spirit if it is to be understood. The apostles understood the truth spoken by the Son because the Spirit revealed it to them. Even their initial faith in the Son was a gift of revelation. Jesus stated it clearly: *"Flesh and blood has not revealed this* [faith] *to you, but My Father who is in heaven"* (Matthew 16:17). Every principle of the kingdom, including the gate of faith, can be known by the revelation of the Holy Spirit, and by no other way.

> *"All things have been delivered to Me by My Father, and no one knows the Son except the Father. Nor does anyone know the Father except the Son,* ***and the one to whom the Son wills to reveal Him."*** MATTHEW 11:27, EMPHASIS ADDED

The Son reveals the Father. The Spirit of the Son has taken up its abode in the human heart and He—the Spirit of truth—reveals all things concerning the Father's Kingdom. These Two Witnesses—Father and Son—are made known to each individual by the testimony of the indwelling Spirit and Word. It is only through the process of revelation that we grow as individual citizens of God's Kingdom. And this is how we continue to progress throughout the court and the Temple: Always it is through the revelation of the mysteries found in Jesus Christ. There are multitudes of believers who dwell only in the court because they have not yet received a revelation of their Temple treasures. To these precious people, the Temple has remained a mystery through no fault of their own. Traditional church teachings have shrouded our Temple inheritance. In this new day, however, God is once again revealing the Temple treasures in all their brilliance.

We must be personally convinced beyond a shadow of doubt of two prerequisite ideas if we are to seek the hidden manna: One, mysteries do exist in the Kingdom of Heaven, and two, God wants to share these mysteries with His people. There are those contemporary Christian assemblies that either deny the existence of spiritual mysteries in God's Kingdom, or else they teach that the mysteries are beyond the domain of our inheritance. These are serious misunderstandings. Mysteries do exist, and God wants His people to understand them.

> *We speak the wisdom of God in a mystery, the hidden wisdom [hidden manna] which God ordained before the ages for our glory.* 1 CORINTHIANS 2:7

In this verse both prerequisite ideas are affirmed. Not only is the wisdom of God hidden in a mystery, but He preordained the wisdom to become our glory. How do we receive these secrets of divine wisdom that God has prepared for those who love Him?

> *God has revealed them to us through His Spirit. For the Spirit searches all things, yes, the deep things of God.* 1 CORINTHIANS 2:10

Revealed ... through His Spirit ... this is how we experience the hidden manna.

> *By revelation He made known to me the mystery ... which in other ages was not made known to the sons of*

men, as it has now been revealed by the Spirit to His holy apostles and prophets. EPHESIANS 3:3, 5

Paul had the awesome awareness that his generation was chosen of God to know spiritual mysteries not known in previous ages. None of the esteemed patriarchs and prophets of the Old Testament knew the mysteries of the kingdom—not Noah, Abraham, Isaiah, Ezekiel, Daniel—no, not even Moses, the man who received the Law and the pattern for the Tabernacle. The mysteries were hidden in Christ from Earth's foundations and were only made known as He was made known in the hearts of mankind. The Son, perfect embodiment of the Spirit of revelation, opened the veil to make known the mysteries of the kingdom. These same mysteries are revealed today as the Word of God is made plain through spiritual enlightenment.

That the God of our Lord Jesus Christ, the Father of glory, may give to you the spirit of wisdom and revelation in the knowledge of Him, the eyes of your understanding being enlightened. EPHESIANS 1:17-18

We have spiritual "*eyes of understanding*" that are enlightened by the Holy Spirit. An apt comparison can be made between natural eyes and eyes of understanding. Our natural eyes cannot see in an environment of total darkness. They are reliant upon an adequate source of light. In the same way, our eyes of understanding must have a source of light in order to perceive. It was Paul's prayer that the Father of glory would give us "*the spirit of wisdom and revelation.*" His Spirit alone provides the light that is essential in order for our eyes of understanding to see.

Consider the terms *reveal* and *revelation.* The root meaning of these terms is *disclosure.* Taken literally, they also convey the bold idea *to take off the cover*. We can approach the hidden manna with these definitions in mind. The hidden manna is the wisdom of God made known through His firstborn Son. The Son is the brilliant radiance of the Father's manifold wisdom. In knowing the Son, therefore, we become partakers of the Father's eternal wisdom. We become heirs together of the Son-light that so graciously illumines our human Temples. It cannot be emphasized enough: The Son reveals the Father. The Son discloses the secrets of the Father's Kingdom. In effect, the Son takes off the cover—the Mercy Seat—so that we can behold the hidden manna and partake of it.

The wisdom of the Father is not a mystery to the Son. Yet it is a mystery to those who have not received their inheritance in the Son. Each facet of divine wisdom is a mystery until it is revealed by the Spirit within the heart of each seeker. Another name for divine wisdom is truth. The Son—the one who is truth—gave a principle of the kingdom when He said this: "*You shall know the truth, and the truth shall make you free*" (John 8:32). To receive revelation of truth is to know the Son more completely. The Son is the Father's personal gift of freedom to each and every human. We receive the gift by faith and begin to fathom its extraordinary implications. The Son, made known to us by degrees of enlightenment, liberates our lives from every form of human bondage. The Son, the truth, the living bread, the Word of God, the hidden manna: This is our miraculous gift.

The golden pot of manna in the Mosaic Tabernacle was representative of the infinite wisdom of God found in Christ. The pot of manna was hid away in the Ark beneath the Mercy Seat in order to direct our attention to the mysteries known only by the Spirit. The Father desires spiritual offspring. It is His will that we grow and develop in spiritual matters—even to the complete comprehension of the mysteries of His Kingdom.

The hidden manna is inside the Temple. If it is inside the Temple, then it is part of our heritage in the Lord. We are the Temple of God and His Spirit dwells within. It is God's intention that we will come to understand all mysteries pertaining to the

Temple of His Son. Full disclosure of truth is the Father's will. He desires to divulge His secrets unto the household of faith. He wants to remove the cover to reveal His glorious treasures. He longs for a family of mature sons and daughters, made to be in the image of His firstborn, with whom He can share the deepest mysteries of His eternal kingdom. The Father loves fellowship with His children in the Spirit. The Temple of the Son gets to the core of the Father's heart. It is the revelation of truth the Son imparted to His disciples two thousand years ago with great power and victory. Now we also are overcomers through Christ who loves us, and He has granted that we can eat of the hidden manna just as His earlier disciples.

> *That sacred mystery which up till now has been hidden in every age and every generation, but which is now as clear as daylight to those who love God. They are those to whom God has planned to give a vision of the full wonder and splendor of his secret plan for the nations. And the secret is simply this: Christ* ***in you****! Yes, Christ* ***in you*** *bringing with him the hope of all the glorious things to come.* Colossians 1:26-27, ph, emphasis added

The mystery of God was hidden throughout every generation and for long ages until the fullness of time when the Son took off the cover, brought full disclosure, and revealed the wisdom of God to mankind. The Father's predestined plan of the ages coalesced in one magnificent secret: Christ in you is the hope of glory!

> *For God's secret plan, now at last made known, is Christ himself. In him lie hidden all the mighty, untapped treasures of wisdom and knowledge.* Colossians 2:2-3, tlb

This hidden, untapped bounty of divine wisdom and knowledge is given full and free expression in Christ—the Anointing—as He dwells richly in the hearts of His people. Certainly we can expect the disclosure of kingdom mysteries as we prayerfully contemplate the Scriptures. "*He* [the Son] *opened their understanding, that they might comprehend the Scriptures*" (Luke 24:45). The Son is made known in our lives when the Word of truth is engrafted by the Spirit to work a mighty transformation in our character. We are changed when we partake of the manna hidden within the pages of the Bible. Rather than just quote the profound principles of the Bible, we also seek out the source of its inspiration. For the same Spirit which inspired the writing of the holy Scriptures now dwells in these human Temples. The Spirit of Christ, combined with His Word of truth, equals the living Word—the Logos. The Logos reveals the mysteries of the kingdom. The Logos makes known the secrets of the Father and Son. The Logos clearly expresses the hidden manna. The Logos becomes our possession when the Spirit opens our understanding so that the written Scriptures become the living Word.

After His Resurrection and glorification, the Son was known among the apostles in a new and transformative way. They knew Him as the Word rather than the physical Son of Man. They realized that the power of the Word that indwelt them was the very same Logos who created the foundations of the Earth. This new and transforming experience brought the Word into clear focus. It was the Word who was made flesh to dwell among men; who manifested the Father's glory through healings, miracles, signs, and wonders; who endured death on the Cross for the salvation and redemption of humanity; who was resurrected from the grave and entered into glorification for the ultimate deliverance of all. This was the Logos, the new inheritance of the apostles. And it is our inheritance today.

The Bible speaks to every realm of the court and the Temple. From the elementary to the profound, the Bible reflects the many-sided diamond of divine wisdom. Two Testaments, both the Old and the New, silently lie upon the table, the bookshelf, or the church podium. We can take these two witnesses in our hands and, with humble attitude and prayerful search, read the written words that testify of the Father and Son. We read the words diligently with our natural eyes and minds; words that we realize hold great depths of revelatory meaning. And then, miraculously, the Spirit opens the eyes of our understanding so that our minds perceive the mysteries of God.

The Old and New Testaments are two witnesses that testify of the Father and Son. When the Spirit of life enters into our reading and meditation, then the two witnesses stand upon their feet in us. The Bible comes alive as the Word walks and talks in human vessels. We receive a clear perception of both the Father and the Son when their spiritual presence—the Holy Spirit—provides the revelation of the Word of truth.

The purpose of the Temple treasures is to bring us into close communion and fellowship with the Father and Son. The revelation of the Temple treasures, including the hidden manna, enriches our spiritual fellowship. "*The grace of the Lord Jesus Christ* [Son], *and the love of God* [Father], *and the* ***communion*** [fellowship] ***of the Holy Spirit*** *be with you all*" (2 Corinthians 13:14, emphasis added). We can have fellowship with the Father and Son as we commune with the Holy Spirit.

> *Truly* ***our fellowship is with the Father and with His Son*** *Jesus Christ.* 1 JOHN 1:3, EMPHASIS ADDED

> *God* [the Father] *is faithful, by whom you were called into* ***the fellowship of His Son****, Jesus Christ our Lord.* 1 CORINTHIANS 1:9, EMPHASIS ADDED

Human beings can have meaningful fellowship with one another whenever good friends are willing to disclose their personal motives and intentions. Lacking disclosure, there remains an unstated mistrust and uncertainty. The fellowship can only go as deep as friends can trust each other and be certain of the other's sincerity. This same condition applies to our fellowship with the Father. He knows our heart, but we can only know His heart through the revelation of His Son. No one can know the Father unless the Son reveals Him, and all revelation is by the Spirit.

The Bible holds the mystery of the Father and Son. Indeed, we need to study the Scriptures. And yet it is equally important to study the Holy Spirit. Observe the Spirit. Meditate upon the Spirit. Offer praise and worship in the Spirit. Pray in the Spirit. Obey the leading of the Spirit. Our communion with the Holy Spirit is the key to open the written mystery of the two witnesses. The Old and New Testaments are quickened to life by the Spirit who originally inspired the writing of them. Behind the printed pages of the Bible stand the Father and Son that no man in his carnal mind can approach nor even perceive. Yet the Father and Son step forth in majesty from the pages of the book when we learn to perceive by the Spirit. The carnal veils, which cover the heart and mind, are taken away in Christ, the Anointing. The veils fall away and we enter sweet fellowship with mysteries held secret for all ages prior to the Son.

> *And to make all see what is* ***the fellowship of the mystery****, which from the beginning of the ages has been hidden in God who created all things through Jesus Christ.*
> EPHESIANS 3:9, EMPHASIS ADDED

God the Father has appointed His firstborn Son as the Captain of our salvation. We honor and love Him as our Savior. He is both the Author and Finisher of our faith. To us He is and always shall be the King of kings and Lord of lords. All foundations and ages were created by the Word—the Logos, the Son. It is only in the Son that we find eternal reason and purpose. In Him we find fellowship with the two witnesses, as the Spirit and Word become the essential character of our inner man. The revelation of the Word through the Spirit is no stranger to the household of God. *"There is a God in heaven who reveals secrets…* " (Daniel 2:28). He elevates His children into heavenly places in Christ Jesus because He loves them and desires that they receive the revelation of His secrets.

Paul referred to this revelatory understanding in the following way: *"I neither received it from man, nor was I taught it, but it came through **the revelation of Jesus Christ**"* (Galatians 1:12, emphasis added). Each individual seeker will grow into maturity in God because of the revelation of Jesus Christ. It is our responsibility to seek, ask, read, study, and listen, but when all is said and done, we must receive the Word by revelation of the Spirit. There is no other way.

> *The anointing which you have received from Him abides in you, and you do not need that anyone teach you … the same anointing teaches you concerning all things.*
> 1 JOHN 2:27

This does not discount the need for God-appointed teachers and ministers. It does, however, emphasize the fact that each of God's children has the right to depend on the anointing of His Spirit to reveal the truth. The anointing ought to be the inspiration of our teachers, and the same Spirit-anointing ought to abide in us. It is the Spirit who quickens; the flesh profits nothing.

The hidden manna is our inheritance. An unlimited supply of the bread of life is reserved in the golden Ark. When we diligently seek out our Temple treasures we will discover this hidden source of divine inspiration that the Father has reserved for those who love Him. Whatever we lack concerning the mysteries of the kingdom *"… God will reveal even this to you"* (Philippians 3:15).

Always remember: Abundant manna is miraculously provided by the Father when we are hungry enough to seek it out, receive it, and eat of it.

HIDDEN MANNA COMES BY REVELATION:
THE ANOINTED WORD GIVES THE EXPLANATION.

AARON'S ROD

Key Word: Authority

Significance

Aaron's rod signifies the God-given authority bestowed on those who have reached maturity in the Melchizedek priesthood. Great responsibility accompanies great authority in God's Kingdom. Aaron's rod, the fulfillment of one's spiritual quest, means graduation with high honors. But it also means that one has been prepared for the Master's use in new and mighty ways—a promotion into higher realms of divine manifestation.

Supportive Scriptures

> *They shall speak of the glory of Your kingdom, and talk of Your power, to make known to the sons of men His mighty acts, and the glorious majesty of His kingdom.* PSALM 145:11-12

> *He taught them as one having authority, and not as the scribes.* MATTHEW 7:29

> *They were astonished at His teaching, for His word was with authority.* LUKE 4:32

"All authority has been given to Me in heaven and on earth." MATTHEW 28:18

He must reign till He has put all enemies under His feet. 1 CORINTHIANS 15:25

"The kingdoms of this world have become the kingdoms of our Lord and of His Christ, and He shall reign forever and ever!" REVELATION 11:15

Do you not know that the saints will judge the world?" 1 CORINTHIANS 6:2

Physical Description

Moses, chosen by God to lead the tribes of Israel, was insecure regarding his own abilities as leader. He also seriously doubted that the Israelites would heed his words. God therefore appointed Aaron as Moses' chief spokesman, and He empowered these two men with the rod of authority.

The rod was simply the sturdy section of an almond branch that Moses carried in his hand. *"So the LORD said to him, 'What is that in your hand?' He* [Moses] *said, 'A rod'"* (Exodus 4:2). The Scriptures then explain how the rod could be transformed into a serpent and back again to a rod. (See Exodus 4:3-4.) The rod became the visible extension, or the outward sign, of the divine authority invested in Moses and Aaron.

God imbued this plain almond branch with wondrous power. *"And you shall take this rod in you hand, with which you shall do the signs"* (Exodus 4:17). These miraculous signs were instrumental in the deliverance of the Israelites from Egyptian bondage. Moses and Aaron, wielding the rod according to God's direct command, brought great plagues upon the Egyptians until Pharaoh finally agreed to let Israel go.

The authority of the rod was again demonstrated when Pharaoh's army pinned the fleeing Israelites against the Red

Sea. At this critical moment of entrapment and apparent hopelessness, God had Moses use the rod to part the waters of the Red Sea.

> *"Tell the children of Israel to go forward. But lift up your rod, and stretch out your hand over the sea and divide it. And the children of Israel shall go on dry ground through the midst of the sea."* EXODUS 14:15-16

After the people of Israel had escaped to safety, Moses caused the heaped waters of the Red Sea to drown Pharaoh's army. This he did by the same authority of the almond branch.

Later, when the people thirsted for lack of water in the wilderness, the Lord told Moses to strike the rock in Horeb "*and water will come out of it*" (Exodus 17:6). The rod was hereby used to provide a miraculous supply of water. In another instance, Moses held up the rod during the time of battle so that Israel prevailed victoriously. Time and again the divine authority of Aaron's rod brought victory in the face of insurmountable odds. It is critical to note that in every instance Moses utilized the rod in strict obedience to God's leadership and command.

Eventually the leaders of the twelve tribes became contentious with Moses and Aaron. This dispute over leadership was settled according to the instructions given by God. God told Moses to have each tribal leader present his own rod with the leader's name inscribed on it.

> *"Then you shall place them in the tabernacle of meeting before the Testimony* [tablets of stone], *where I meet with you. And it shall be that the rod of the man whom I choose will blossom...." Now it came to pass on the next day that Moses went into the tabernacle of witness, and behold, the rod of Aaron, of the house of Levi, had sprouted and put forth buds, had produced blossoms and yielded ripe almonds.... And the LORD said to Moses,*

> *"Bring Aaron's rod back before the Testimony, to be kept as a sign...."* NUMBERS 17:4-5, 8, 10

Aaron's rod was given this decisive display of divine favor. In this way Aaron's rod was appointed by God to find its ultimate resting place in the golden Ark in the Holy of Holies.

Spiritual Application

Aaron's rod represents divine authority. Yet the story of the rod's origin directs us in the way of humility and obedience. Consider the man Moses. *"Now the man Moses was very humble* [meek], *more than all men who were on the face of the earth"* (Numbers 12:3). Moses did not esteem himself capable, or worthy, to be ruler of Israel. It was God who exalted Moses into leadership, and it was God who empowered the almond branch as the visible emblem of Moses' authority. A man of meekness, combined with a humble wooden branch; this is not an image that evokes an aura of authority. But this unique combination became dynamic once empowered by Almighty God.

God exalted Moses into leadership when he was eighty years old. His life was carefully orchestrated by God for maximum character development. Lessons of humility graced his pathway. During his eighty years of intense preparation, Moses endured the humbling experiences of broken pride, shattered personal dreams, and the realization of personal weaknesses and limitations. A man of meekness holding up a simple branch from an almond tree suited God's purposes perfectly. The Word of God sums it up quite well: *"'Not by might nor by power, but by My Spirit,' says the LORD of hosts"* (Zechariah 4:6).

> *Where is the wise? Where is the scribe? Where is the disputer of this age? Has not God made foolish the wisdom of this world?... For you see your calling, brethren, that not many wise according to the flesh, not*

> *many mighty, not many noble, are called. But God has chosen the foolish things of the world to put to shame the wise, and God has chosen the weak things of the world to put to shame the things which are mighty; and the base things of the world and the things which are despised God has chosen, and the things which are not, to bring to nothing the things that are, that no flesh should glory in His presence.* 1 CORINTHIANS 1:20, 26-29

Moses learned to glory in the Lord. His obedience to the Lord's leadership became the strength of his character. In the context of his daily life, he looked for God's guidance and assistance in all things. He listened for the Word of the Lord in the face of complex challenges because He trusted God's Word above all human voices. Moses' humility before God, combined with his obedience to God, were the essential prerequisites to his divine empowerment. These two attributes, humility and obedience unto God, foreshadowed Jesus Christ.

Moses prophesied of the Savior:

> *Moses truly said to the fathers, "The LORD your God will raise up for you a Prophet* ***like me*** *from your brethren. Him you shall hear in all things."* ACTS 3:22, EMPHASIS ADDED

Jesus, like Moses, exemplified humility and obedience. He did not seek His own human will but that of His heavenly Father. He did not exalt himself among men, but always spoke the words and did the deeds pleasing to the Father. The apparent contradiction between humility and authority found resolution in both Moses and Christ. The Savior truthfully spoke of His own authority: *"All things have been delivered to Me by My Father..."* (Matthew 11:27), and again, *"All power is given unto me in heaven and in earth"* (Matthew 28:18, KJV). Yet in His daily life He exuded the virtues of humility, compassion, and love rather than arrogance.

> *"Come to Me, all you who labor and are heavy laden, and I will give you rest. Take My yoke upon you and learn from Me, for I am gentle [meek] and lowly in heart, and you will find rest for your souls. For My yoke is easy and My burden is light."* MATTHEW 11:28-30

Our Savior is the embodiment of the Temple treasures, including Aaron's rod. We must recognize in Him both the Lamb of God (priesthood) *and* the Lion of the tribe of Judah (kingship). He tenderly healed the afflicted and fed the hungry multitudes. Yet He also rebuked the prideful religious leaders, denounced the lies and hypocrisy of the old religious establishment, and with great boldness confronted the moneychangers in the Temple, overthrowing their tables and driving them out with a homemade whip. The Lamb and the Lion were not contradictions. Rather they were two integral aspects of the divine nature.

The Son of God, the epitome of divine authority, willingly submitted His holy life to the Cross for the salvation of the world. He endured the Cross because of the joy that was set before Him. The joy was the inheritance. His fullness of joy was only attainable through crucifixion and resurrection. His obedience to the Father's will was the catalyst that activated the fullness of His divine inheritance as King of kings and Lord of lords. We need to recognize the joy that is set before us. Our own inheritance in Christ is based entirely upon His kingship and lordship. Our Temple treasures are secured only in the Son. The more we uphold the Son of God the more we behold our magnificent heritage in Him. The revelation of Jesus Christ in our earthen vessels brings great humility and obedience. When the revelation of the Son illumines our souls with the pristine, golden treasures of our inheritance, we joyfully submit our will in obedience to God.

> *To Him who loved us and washed us from our sins in His own blood, and has made us kings and priests to His God and Father, to Him be glory and dominion forever and ever.* REVELATION 1:5-6

We cannot deny what He has made us to be: kings and priests. He is the King *of kings.* He is the Lord *of lords.* We are made to be kings and priests as we are transformed into the image and likeness of the Son. We grow up in Him in all things. We grow in grace and knowledge. We gain maturity through fiery trials, and we are seasoned by those things we suffer. We emerge triumphant in His resurrection life as we learn to overcome by exercising His Spirit and Word. We put truth into action in our daily lives.

The Apostle Peter declared that God's called-out people are *"...a royal priesthood"* (1 Peter 2:9). Peter and the other apostles experienced this realm of divine authority. *"And with **great power** the apostles gave witness to the resurrection of the Lord Jesus. And **great grace** was upon them all"* (Acts 4:33, emphasis added). As we read the Book of Acts and study the apostles' writings, it becomes apparent that the apostles entered into their own Temple treasures. As eyewitnesses of the Lord's majesty, they knew to go beyond the court into the depths of the Temple. Here, in the Holy Places not made by hands, they received great grace and power. They humbled themselves to the leadership of the Savior while He dwelt among them in the flesh. Just as importantly, they humbled themselves to the power of His Spirit and the authority of His Word after He ascended into glory.

Humility is a principle of the kingdom. It is a point of emphasis in both the Old and New Testaments.

Before honor is humility. PROVERBS 15:33

The LORD is near to those who have a broken heart, and saves such as have a contrite spirit. PSALM 34:18

The sacrifices of God are a broken spirit, a broken and a contrite heart—these, O God, You will not despise. PSALM 51:17

Yes, all of you be submissive to one another, and be clothed with humility, for "God resists the proud, but gives grace to the humble." 1 PETER 5:5

"Whoever exalts himself will be humbled, and he who humbles himself will be exalted." LUKE 14:11

Our Savior spoke the above principle, and He demonstrated its transformational power. *"He* ***humbled*** *Himself and became* ***obedient*** *to the point of death, even the death of the cross. Therefore God also has highly exalted Him and given Him the name which is above every name"* (Philippians 2:8-9, emphasis added). The Son, known as the Word of God, came from Heaven to dwell among men; that is, He humbled himself in order to live and suffer as a man. As the living Word, He was obedient to the will and purpose of the Father, even to submit to the humiliation of death on the Cross. The Father, true to His Word, highly exalted the Word.

Jesus, the Word made flesh, was the Temple. The Temple spoke truth principles so that all mankind would gain access to their own Temple inheritance. Belief in the truth not only opens the Temple, but also establishes the Temple treasures in the seeker's life. The Temple is not a form of religious mysticism. Nor is it attainable through human philosophy or religious works. The Temple is established upon the rock-solid foundational principles of eternal truth.

In essence, we could say that the blueprint is the Bible and the foundation is the Son. We cannot sidestep the truth principles of the kingdom nor escape their governance if we hope to experience our full Temple heritage. The beauty of the Temple built on truth is that it innately rules self out. The self-nature can manipulate earthly religion for carnal purposes, but the self-nature has no place, no rule, no power, and no inheritance in the Temple of the Son.

Jesus promised that the truth will make us free. Truth is composed of many Kingdom principles. As each principle of truth is written within our heart and mind, we are freed from the bondage of self. Truth becomes paramount, rather than human personality, in the Temple of the Son. Truth protects our divine inheritance like a flaming sword. It turns every way to protect the tree of life—the Temple treasures. We cannot have the treasures of resurrection life unless we go through the flaming sword.

Consider the flaming sword: It is the Word of God empowered by the Spirit. Our passage through the flaming sword purges out everything that would bring deception and corruption into the Temple and the kingdom. The Word of truth (the sword) and the Spirit of truth (the flame) are indivisible, and their eternal unity of design and purpose purges us from all sin. Indeed, the flaming sword is integrated into every aspect of both the court and the Temple. We enter in by faith in the Son, and we are made free by our passage through His truth and His Spirit. Providing full access to the Temple, including Aaron's rod, is the highest honor the Father could bestow on His offspring. *"No man takes this honor to himself, but he who is called by God, just as Aaron was"* (Hebrews 5:4).

Recall the humble almond branch in Moses' hand in consideration of the Son. God highly exalted the natural branch to become Aaron's rod. Aaron's rod swallowed all opposing serpents, wrought plagues against Egypt, parted the Red Sea, produced water from the rock, brought victory in war, and then miraculously budded, flowered, and bore almonds. God exalted Aaron's rod, that simple and inconspicuous almond branch, into a dynamic symbol of divine authority. If the mighty authority of Aaron's rod were made manifest today, it would inspire fearsome awe among the people.

Aaron's rod, a key component in the original Tabernacle built by Moses, points us to the authority and power inherent in Jesus Christ. More than this, it directs our attention to the Temple in which Christ dwells—His people. Aaron's rod, like all other aspects of the court and Temple, is not some alien object far off in the distant heavens, nor is it buried in some lost archeological ruins. It dwells within every child of God as a hidden spiritual treasure. It is one aspect of "*...Christ in you, the hope of glory...* (Colossians 1:27), and this anointed inheritance will not fail in its expression of spiritual authority. The ultimate authority of the Son has not yet been fully manifested in the lives of His people, although the disciples certainly experienced it in a measure two thousand years ago.

Aaron's rod, as a physical almond branch, symbolized the Branch that we know as our Savior, Lord, and King. The Old Testament prophets wrote of the coming Messiah, and they often referred to Him as the Branch. The following verses help make the connection between Aaron's rod and the Son of God:

> *There shall come forth a Rod from the stem of Jesse, and a Branch shall grow out of his roots. The Spirit of the LORD shall rest upon Him.* ISAIAH 11:1-2

> *In that day the Branch of the LORD shall be beautiful and glorious.* ISAIAH 4:2

> *Behold, I am bringing forth My Servant the BRANCH.* ZECHARIAH 3:8

> *Behold, the days are coming, says the LORD, that I will raise to David a Branch of righteousness; a King shall reign and prosper, and execute judgment and righteousness in the earth.... Now this is His name by which He will be called: THE LORD OUR RIGHTEOUSNESS.* JEREMIAH 23:5-6

Truly, the Branch was revealed in the person of the Messiah, the Anointed One. Among His many titles and names, certainly one of the Savior's most endearing names is The Lord Our Righteousness. As the King of kings, He does reign and prosper, and He shall indeed execute judgment and righteousness in the Earth. Jesus fulfilled these Old Testament prophecies. He exemplifies the authority of Aaron's rod.

There is an apt comparison to be made between the almond branch carried by Moses and the Christ child born in a manger and raised in the unassuming lifestyle of a carpenter's son. Both branches evoke humility. The Branch, Jesus, did not appeal to human eyes. He did not fit the carnal expectations of organized religion. He was too common, too plain, too humble, and His teachings were too unconventional. It certainly appeared to the leaders of Israel that the Branch did not meet their standards and preconceived notions of the Messiah. The Branch, in fact, was violently rejected by the religious establishment.

The religious leaders of Israel searched the Old Testament Scriptures hoping to find eternal life in the patterns. The patterns, however, were merely symbols of the glory that were yet to be revealed in the Son. As worldly wise, sophisticated scholars, the Pharisees and Sadducees diligently pored over the Scriptures that described the Mosaic Tabernacle. Confined to the types-and-shadows of the Law Covenant, they thrilled to the Scriptures that told the story of the almond branch called Aaron's rod. They marveled at the power and authority that emanated from the almond branch. Yet they rejected and denounced the Branch of Righteousness when He stood in their midst. They loved the patterns—the shadows—but not the true light.

Today we recognize the Branch as our Savior, and our faith in the Son creates deliverance and transformation in our lives. However, the spiritual significance of the Branch goes even deeper when we realize that the Branch of the Lord dwells within these earthly vessels. It is the indwelling Branch who establishes divine authority from beyond the veil. This is an authority of kingship and priesthood that emanates from the one whose name is above every name in Heaven and Earth.

The authority of His name is much more than letters and words on the printed page. Rather, His name is the divine nature of the Father revealed in His Son so that mankind can learn to draw upon the new life of the Spirit. We can learn to walk in His name, to speak in His name, and to pray in His name once we realize that the Branch of righteousness is our inheritance. We call upon His name, not as a formula of words, but as the very nature of the Son—His authority as both King and Lord.

We must ask ourselves: Who is the Son? Our response identifies the meaning of His name. Name Him: He is life, light, love, peace, joy, righteousness, truth, wisdom, knowledge, understanding, power, dominion, and glory. His name is manifold. *Manifold* means "many-sided, or multidimensional." The Son is the radiant, universal diamond with an infinite number of fine-hewed glistening facets. Each facet of the Son reflects another dimension of our heavenly Father. Each facet is another aspect of the Son's name.

The Branch emanates authority. He possessed divine authority when He dwelt on Earth two thousand years ago, but He was not appointed by the Father to be made into an earthly king with a natural domain. Multitudes of people saw the Son's miracles and healings and would have made Him their king. In spite of this human adulation and the possibilities of a tremendous earthly kingdom, the Son recognized the higher calling of the Cross, the Resurrection, and the glorification of a kingdom not of this world. Therefore, He submitted His human will to the Father's will.

The Father's plan was far greater than one individual Son sitting on a throne ruling over the Earth. It was the Father's intention to exalt His Son as King of kings and Lord of lords—the firstborn of many brethren. This exaltation would not be of earthly substance or of the human domain. Instead the Son would be exalted in the Spirit, in the Kingdom of Heaven, and in the temple not made by human hands. The Son, facing crucifixion, said it plainly: *"If My kingdom were of this world, My servants would fight…"* (John 18:36). The Son relinquished His personal rights to an earthly kingdom in order to establish the far-reaching goals of the heavenly kingdom. His spiritual kingship was forever linked to the heritage of the complete family of God. Indeed, the Father ordained every member of His household of faith to be a spiritual heir in the Kingdom of the Son forever free from earthly limitations.

The Father's plan of the ages was exceedingly brilliant: Let every human receive the ultimate opportunity to enter the court through the gate of faith and thereby proceed into the fullness of their Temple treasures. Let Christ and the entirety of His Kingdom and Temple become the inheritance of humankind.

> *To the Son He* [the Father] *says: "Your throne, O God, is forever and ever; a scepter of righteousness is the scepter of Your kingdom. You have loved righteousness and hated lawlessness; therefore God, Your God, has anointed You with the oil of gladness more than Your companions."* HEBREWS 1:8-9

The Father anointed the Son with an eternal throne of authority in the kingdom founded upon righteousness. The kingdom is inhabited by multitudes who believe in the Son, trust Him as the Word, and love the righteousness established through His Kingship and Lordship. We are thankful to be the companions of the firstborn Son. Our hearts rejoice with the realization that we are brothers and sisters of the firstborn Son—our Elder Brother. The Word declares we are heirs of God and joint-heirs of Christ. It is this heritage that creates a deep inner longing for His Kingdom to be manifested in the Earth. Indeed, His Spirit within us cries out for a greater expression of righteousness in our personal lives and in human society. The redeemed soul groans for the manifestation of His righteousness in fullness of power and authority.

> *Behold, a king will reign in righteousness, and princes will rule with justice.* Isaiah 32:1

Humanity longs for a righteous and just government. There is a universal desire for the Kingdom of Heaven. Our new birth as citizens of God's Kingdom does not diminish but rather increases the desire that His righteousness flow like a river in the midst of the human family. This call to destiny—a spiritual fire in the belly—is the relentless urge of the Spirit of God. It urges His Kingdom to come forth in all of its power and glory. This urge of the Spirit for righteous government is ordained of God to break forth in our time. With unbounded power it overflows all human walls of carnal division, separation, and dissension. Its very heart beats with the blood of redemption, and its every breath inhales the Holy Spirit of Almighty God and his Son. The will of God is that His kingdom take dominion of a troubled planet, and this heavenly unction burns like a pillar of fire and hovers like a cloud of glory within the Temple of God's people.

Jesus provided a deep insight: *"The kingdom ... is within you..."* (Luke 17:21). The Lord's Kingdom dwells in the hearts of His people in every city and in every nation. The Day Star of this revelation arises in the life of every sincere seeker. It dawns on us that we are citizens of God's eternal kingdom. The realization that we are members of the Melchizedek Order refreshes us like the break of a new day. The haze of stagnated religious traditions opens to the light of day to reveal our High Priest ruling with a golden scepter of righteousness. Now we see Him clearly as both King of peace and King of righteousness.

The Kingdom of God is our kingdom. The Melchizedek Order is our order. The life of the resurrection is the birth of our new day. We are heirs together of the grace of life and we cannot help but love righteousness and hate iniquity. We are in the world—its earthly kingdoms and orders—but we are born of the Spirit and Word into a higher kingdom and a superior order. *Abba Father!* We cry it out with tears of joy. The universal cry goes forth from the human breast: "Thy Kingdom come and Thy will be done on Earth as it is in Heaven."

> *And in the days of these* [earthly] *kings the God of heaven will set up a* [heavenly] *kingdom which shall never be destroyed; and the kingdom shall not be left to other people; it shall break in pieces and consume all these kingdoms, and it shall stand forever.* DANIEL 2:44

> *Then the kingdom and dominion, and the greatness of the kingdoms under the whole heaven, shall be given to the people, the saints of the Most High. His kingdom is an everlasting kingdom, and all dominions shall serve and obey Him.* DANIEL 7:27

Every promise of God shall be fulfilled. Take careful notice: The promise that God's Kingdom will rule on Earth is to be accomplished through His people. The kingdom and its complete dominion shall be given to the saints of the Most High. The authority of the kingdom shall not be left to other people, but it shall be established in the Temple of the Son and those who dwell therein.

In our consideration of divine authority, the location of Aaron's rod is vital. Aaron's rod is not located in the court, nor is it found in the Holy Place. It is reserved and protected within the golden Ark in the Holy of Holies. Its placement in the Ark of the Covenant magnifies the symbolic value of Aaron's rod. Aaron's rod is an integral aspect of our kingdom inheritance, and it is an essential aspect of our Temple treasures. However, its full expression is made known in those seekers who gain maturity in God. Aaron's rod is the divine authority that is made available when we progress through the court, through the Holy Place, and into the Holy of Holies. The authority of the Lord—the Branch—is manifested in overcomers.

> *"And he who overcomes, and keeps My works until the end, to him I will give power over the nations—'He shall rule them with a rod of iron; they shall be dashed to pieces like the potter's vessels'—as I* [the Son] *also have received from My Father."* REVELATION 2:26-27

As previously explained, we grow and prosper in God's Kingdom through humility and obedience to Him. Our primary objective is not to rule over other people but to rule well over our own house, or Temple. We overcome every carnal challenge by walking in the Spirit and Word. We learn to keep His works, the Temple treasures, until we reach the end, or the main goal, which is spiritual maturity. The learning process is a spiritual cross that imparts great victory over the self-nature. We experience the invisible cross of the Holy Spirit on a daily basis. The Spirit-walk—the cross—instills lessons of humility and obedience unto the King of kings and Lord of lords.

"For the message of the cross is foolishness to those who are perishing, but to us who are being saved ***it is the power of God****"* (1 Corinthians 1:18, emphasis added). The Cross is the power of God! The power of His Spirit crosses out our self-nature. *"God forbid that I should boast except in the cross of our Lord Jesus Christ, by whom the world has been crucified to me, and I to the world"* (Galatians 6:14). The man and woman who

experience the power of the Cross are being qualified to receive the divine authority of Aaron's rod.

Call to mind the special quality of meekness in the characters of Moses and Christ. As representatives of God's family, we want His divine nature to become reality in our personal Temple. The power of the Cross crucifies the law of sin and death during the days of our regeneration. The end result is that we will use the rod of authority only in obedience to the principles of our Father's Kingdom. The power of the Cross, the power of the Resurrection, the Spirit-walk: this is the victory that overcomes the world.

Our allegiance to the Son is absolute, for in Him we discover the promised land of our God-given inheritance. When Israel entered the Promised Land of Canaan in ancient times, God instructed them to conquer the ungodly nations that inhabited the land. Today we take spiritual authority over the promised land of our inheritance in Christ. All nations of the self-nature in our promised land are foreign to Him and are thereby conquered. With the rod of His authority we proclaim the victory and dominion over the nations of carnality that once held our hearts and minds in bondage.

The following verses portray the authority of Aaron's rod as it is manifested through the Son and all those who enter the fullness of the Temple of the Son.

> *I will declare the decree: the LORD has said to Me, "You are My Son, today I have begotten You. Ask of Me, and I will give You the nations for Your inheritance, and the ends of the earth for Your possession. You shall break them with a rod of iron; You shall dash them to pieces like a potter's vessel."* PSALM 2:7-9

> *Now out of His mouth goes a sharp sword [of truth], that with it He should strike the nations. And He Himself will rule them with a rod of iron.... And He has*

> *on His robe and on His thigh a name written: KING OF KINGS AND LORD OF LORDS.* REVELATION 19:15-16

> *These will make war with the Lamb, and the Lamb will overcome them, for He is Lord of lords and King of kings; and those who are with Him are called, chosen, and faithful.* REVELATION 17:14

Those who are with Him! Behold the Father's great family of sons and daughters. The firstborn Son of God is not alone for He has made us to be kings and priests in His Kingdom. We are tried and tested in the fires of adversity to emerge more than conquerors through Christ who loves us.

Multitudes of anointed people are awakened to the dawn of this new day. The arising of the Son floods the Temple with light, glory, and power. No longer a mystery, Aaron's rod is revealed as the authority of God made manifest among men.

THE DIVINE AUTHORITY OF AARON'S ROD:
IT IS THE HERITAGE OF THE CHILDREN OF GOD.

Conclusion

TEMPLE INSIGHT

Insight: Possess Your Temple Heritage

The Mosaic pattern for the court and Tabernacle is a symbolic code that conveys the fullness of our inheritance in Christ. The pattern—which consists of the court, the Holy Place, and the Holy of Holies—reveals the good news we freely receive through faith in the Son of God. Truly, we inherit vast spiritual treasure in these earthen Temples such that the power of Spirit and truth is of God and not of ourselves. In this book we have earnestly explored the depths of the riches of wisdom found in Christ, and every discovered treasure is ours to possess by faith. The Temple of the Son is the Father's gift to us. He desires that we enter into this promised land of divine heritage.

Insight: Identify With the Blueprint

Each aspect, or vessel, of the court and Tabernacle was constructed according to the pattern shown to Moses. God provided not only the necessary instructions, but also the skilled artisans and craftsmen who were anointed to transform the pattern into visible, material form. Equally important, all aspects and vessels had to be properly placed in their respective order in accordance with the pattern. Proper placement of each vessel was as important as its accurate construction. In other words, there is a divine order that governs spiritual advancement through the court, Holy Place, and Holy of Holies. Our knowledge of this divine order greatly facilitates our growth and maturity in Him.

We need to pay attention to the details of the pattern. Please note: The Tabernacle was placed inside the court, not vice versa. The Ark of the Covenant was placed in the Holy of Holies, not in the court. The brazen altar was just inside the gate of faith for a critical reason. The pattern, or design, is a revelation of the divine order that governs the Kingdom of Heaven.

How can we enter into our inheritance if we do not know what it is or where it is located? God has provided a pattern, a map, a chart, a blueprint—a divine order—that will guide us to our full inheritance. But we must learn to read the map, to decipher the chart, to appreciate the details of the blueprint—indeed, to crack the symbolic code of the God-given pattern. God desires mature sons and daughters who understand His order. He wants His offspring to learn their way around His grand and holy habitation. He wants to *show the house to the house* so that all may know their present spiritual location. Just as important, it is God's intent that we continue our exploration and growth in His Temple. Once we understand the treasures that dwell within these Temples not made by hands, we will diligently seek out their full expression and manifestation.

Insight: Experience Teamed With Principle

Each facet of the Temple treasures is both an experience and a principle. In order to truly possess a spiritual treasure, we must experience it. Once experienced, it becomes a principle in our lives that yields continuous blessings and benefits.

The following example will illustrate the mutually supportive roles of experience and principle:

> We can hear about salvation found only in the Son of God, and we can read the tremendous promises of God

recorded in the New Testament. As we ponder and theorize the possibilities of salvation, we stand before the gate of faith just outside the court. We see the gate in front of us. We have some awareness that it offers entrance into the court, but the wonder of salvation remains a mystery until we take that step of faith. We must personally experience faith as the free gift of God's grace. Belief in the Son brings new birth and we enter the court through the gate of faith. We experience salvation, the grace and truth found in the Savior, and this new birth opens unto us the magnificent inheritance of all Temple treasures. This beginning experience of faith is reinforced by the principle of faith. The principle, drawn from the inspired pages of the Bible, is written by the Spirit in our hearts and minds. The *experience* of faith transforms our life, and the *principle* of faith provides a sure foundation upon which we can stand throughout life's many tests and trials.

This solid, unbeatable teamwork between experience and principle applies to all aspects of the court and the Temple.

Insight: The Court Is Part of the Treasure

The court is much larger than the Tabernacle and encompasses it. Ever present in our lives, the court serves as a protective buffer around the sacred treasures of the Temple. The court's prominence in size, and the way in which it shelters the Tabernacle, indicate its essential role.

Vast numbers of believers abide in the gracious accommodations of the court. It is where we all begin our spiritual walk by faith. Every newborn babe in Christ relies upon the court for their elementary instruction in the Lord. The court's foundational influences are vital in every believer's life. The court, when properly established, is a beautiful place to be in God. It is a realm that initiates rapid growth. The Lord abounds in our lives with all grace and knowledge as we are made ready to enter the Temple.

We do not need to linger long in the court prior to our entrance into the Temple. In fact, we can enter the Temple immediately once we believe in the Savior. We can enter the Holy of Holies to sit on the Mercy Seat between the cherubim and therein receive the baptism of the Holy Spirit. This was a common, and expected, occurrence in the virgin Church of two thousand years ago. Newborn believers were baptized in water *and* sealed with the Holy Spirit of promise. The gift of Spirit baptism accompanied the gift of faith.

The opportunity to receive the gift of Spirit baptism in the Holy of Holies is available today. Our inheritance in the Temple of the Son is no less than the apostles and early disciples. The believer, overwhelmed (baptized) by the Spirit of the resurrection, overflows with joy unspeakable and full of glory. Those who have this cherubim experience will soon realize that they cannot consistently remain in the Holy of Holies. In time, the heightened sense of spiritual joy dissipates and the believer leaves the Holy of Holies to re-enter the Holy Place followed by the court. There is a fundamental growth and maturity that must take place in each individual's life. God has provided the court, along with the Holy Place, to sustain the maturation process over the long haul.

It is crucial that believers learn to identify the role of the court in their daily lives. This identification with the court will also make clear the necessity to explore the Temple. We must not neglect the treasures within the Temple if we truly desire to know the Lord and the power of His Resurrection. There is an ultimate calling to become a pillar in the Temple. Our walk in Spirit and truth teaches us to remain steadfast in the Holy Place, but we never want to diminish the essential value of the court. The court is and always will be a key aspect of the pattern revealed to Moses. We are not called to level off in the court, but neither are we to be deluded to think we can live without the court. The complete pattern reveals our heritage in the Son as we are transformed into His likeness.

Insight: A Well-balanced Temple

The Holy of Holies is available at all times, but we do not abide there on a regular, daily basis. The veil into the Holy of Holies is rent in twain so that we have open access to approach the throne of grace with boldness. We can enter into this profoundly deep realm of the presence of God as His Spirit bids. However, it is a misconception to conclude that our daily aim is to dwell in the Holy of Holies. There is a healthy balance in the things of God. We need to learn our way around the court, the Holy Place, and the Holy of Holies—become well acclimated with our divine inheritance—and thereby achieve inner balance by utilizing all aspects of the pattern.

To enter the Holy of Holies is a very special occasion in our walk with the Lord. But we go in and come out according to the will and purpose of God. Jesus, our example and leader, ministered from all three realms. He fulfilled the Law; in particular, He fulfilled the pattern of both the court and Tabernacle. In Him we behold the manifestation of the Spirit in perfect equilibrium, a fine-tuned balance wherein all aspects of the pattern-Son function in harmonious power and authority. *"For He whom God has sent speaks the words of God, for God does not give the Spirit by measure"* (John 3:34). The term *measure* means *a limited portion.* The Son did not operate with a limited portion of Spirit. In other words, He was not an imbalanced Temple of God. He did not confine or slant His ministry, but rather gave fullness of expression.

Jesus did not limit the Spirit to a small measure, or a limited portion. Instead, the Savior demonstrated the harmonious structure of all three realms. As the fully manifested Temple of God—the completeness of the pattern—the Son revealed glorious salvation and deliverance as the light of the world. Now

He has appointed us to be the light-bearers of His brilliantly balanced Temple.

There is enough enlightenment, power, and victory in the Holy Place to sustain us the majority of the time. The Holy of Holies is open and available. Its mighty influence shines through the rent veil into the Holy Place. And, as mentioned, we have the large and spacious court that encompasses and shelters our sacred inner treasures. God provides the reality of the spiritual pattern from the gate to the Ark and everything in between. Nothing of our inheritance in Christ is ever lost. The court, the Holy Place, and the Holy of Holies will always serve us well throughout our earthly journey. The pattern overflows with abundant grace to highly anoint these three distinctive, beautifully integrated, realms.

Insight: Seek Out the Gold

God made a clear distinction between the court and the Temple by the choice of metals. The court's signature metal is brass. Brass is certainly good; we need the brass. It is not to be disdained. However, the Temple's signature metal is gold. Gold greatly exceeds brass in value. God has provided spiritual gold—much more precious than the natural gold that dignified the Mosaic Tabernacle. We are called of God to enter the Holy Places of the Temple to receive this golden inheritance. And, once again, we perceive the mutually supportive value of both the brass and the gold.

Insight: Explore Heavenly Places

The Mosaic Tabernacle, which was located in the center of the court, was easily identifiable, for the Tabernacle stood twice as tall as the court curtain and was covered by badger skins. The beautiful white linen of the court curtain contrasted sharply with the rough animal hides that draped the Tabernacle. Recall that the court was open to the sky whereas the Tabernacle was enclosed. These details have meaning.

In comparison to the spacious court, the Tabernacle was relatively small. Its fifteen-foot height, however, made it a conspicuous object that could be seen by the twelve tribes of Israel in their widespread encampment. The Tabernacle's height causes us to consider the heavenly places we can experience in Christ—the anointed realm within the Temple. Limited in physical space and separated from public scrutiny, the attention of the priest inside the Tabernacle was focused on quality of experience and deep significance rather than mere quantity. The golden light of the candlestick reflected off the tall, vertical, gold-clad boards as it gently lit the intricately embroidered, royally colored linen. Looking upward in prayer, the priest could see cherubim floating in the intricate needlework of blue, purple, and scarlet cloth.

The Temple takes us to new and greater heights in both the Spirit and the Word. In the Temple we find our lives are hid with Christ in God. We are shut in with God in a secret place. The Temple is not as concerned with external activity as it is with profound spiritual relationship. Whereas the court is open to the natural elements, the Temple offers a spiritual environment with no variableness or shadow of turning. The Holy Spirit saturates the Temple with the true rest that remains for the people of God.

The inner golden beauty of the Tabernacle was hidden by the thick layers of animal hides. Goat hair curtains covered the inner linen curtains. This was followed by a layer of rams' skins dyed red. The outer covering of badger skins added to the shelter and seclusion of the priest within the Tabernacle, but also created an external, visual image that was at once both drab and unappealing.

The natural eye, looking upon the badger skins, could not discern the inner beauty and glory of the Tabernacle. So it is with God's people. The Temple treasures are hid in earthen vessels. The glory is of God's Spirit and not dependent on our humanness. *"Not by might nor by power, but by My Spirit, says the LORD of hosts"* (Zechariah 4:6). If our hope is limited to the outer religious man, then we are stuck with badger skins. We must perceive by the Spirit the work of the Spirit in each and every child of God.

Insight: Go Deeper

Recall that the gate of the court faced due east. The normal progression through the court and Temple, therefore, was from east to west. Jesus built upon this symbolic lesson: *"For as the lightning comes from the east and shines as far as the west, so will be the coming of the Son of man"* (Matthew 24:27, RSV). In other words, the revelation of the Son increases as we progress from the gate of the court to the golden Ark of the Holy of Holies. We rejoice in the dawning of the Son-light at the gate, but the full revelation of His glory and grace is not found there. We must move forward. We must go deeper. We must grow and mature until the fullness of the Son-light shines within.

The goal is not to dwell forever at the gate of faith. The goal is to progress through the entire court so that we can enter the Temple. The court is vital and it will always remain foundational in our spiritual journey. We will always treasure the first rays of the dawning of the resurrection morning in our life. However, our entrance through the gate into the court is meant to be foundational in the sense that we are to keep building, keep moving, and keep growing in grace and knowledge. We are to grow up in the Son in all things—and the *all things* are not confined to the court.

It is a new day in God. We are anointed to reestablish the divine order of God so that His people today can experience the court, the Holy Place, and the Holy of Holies in their pure state. Let the confusions of the past fall aside as the pattern burns bright with fiery clarity. Let God reveal His Temple treasures in majestic glory and power.

Appendix

Bible Translations

It is a great resource to have access to such finely honed Bible translations. The following translations were quoted and/or utilized as reference tools in the writing of this book. The use of a variety of Bible translations offers depth of insight and fresh perspective.

AMP *The Amplified Bible*
Grand Rapids: Zondervan (1965)

CB *The Companion Bible*
London, Great Britain: Samuel Bagster & Sons Limited (1972)

CLNT *Concordant Literal New Testament*
Saugus, CA: Concordant Publishing Concern (1966)

CEV *Contemporary English Version*
New York: American Bible Society (1995)

EDNT *Emphatic Diaglott New Testament*
New York: International Bible Students Association (1942)

KJV	*King James Version* Cambridge, Great Britain: University Printing House
TLB	*The Living Bible Paraphrased New Testament* Wheaton, IL: Tyndale House Publishers (1971)
MSG	*The Message: The Bible in Contemporary Language* Colorado Springs: NavPress (2002)
NKJV	*New King James Version* Nashville: Thomas Nelson Publishers (1988)
NAB	*New American Bible* Chicago: Catholic Press (1970)
NASB	*New American Standard Bible* Anaheim, CA: Foundation Press (1973)
NEB	*The New English Bible* New York: Cambridge University Press (1971)
NIV	*New International Version* Colorado Springs: International Bible Society (1978, 1984)
NJB	*New Jerusalem Bible* Garden City, NY: Doubleday (1985)
NLT	*New Living Translation* Wheaton, IL: Tyndale House Publishers (1996)
PH	*New Testament in Modern English* by J.B. Phillips New York: Macmillan (1972)

RSV *Revised Standard Version of the New Testament*
New York: Thomas Nelson & Sons (1971)

TEV *Today's English Version*
New York: American Bible Society (1992)

YLT *Young's Literal Translation* by Robert Young
Grand Rapids: Baker Book House (1898)

ZPNT *Zondervan Parallel New Testament in Greek and English*
Grand Rapids: Zondervan Bible Publishers (1975)

6
E
L
N
D
J
J
R
I II S
I II K
I II C
E N
E
J
P
P
E
S
I
J
L
E
D
H
J
A
O
J
H
Z

bunting and baserunning

text/Paul J. Deegan
illustrations/
Harold Henriksen

Consultant: Jean McCarthy, B.S., University of Minnesota; M.S., Physical Education, Washington State University; Associate Professor of Physical Education and Head Baseball Coach, Mankato State College.

CREATIVE EDUCATION
Mankato, Minnesota

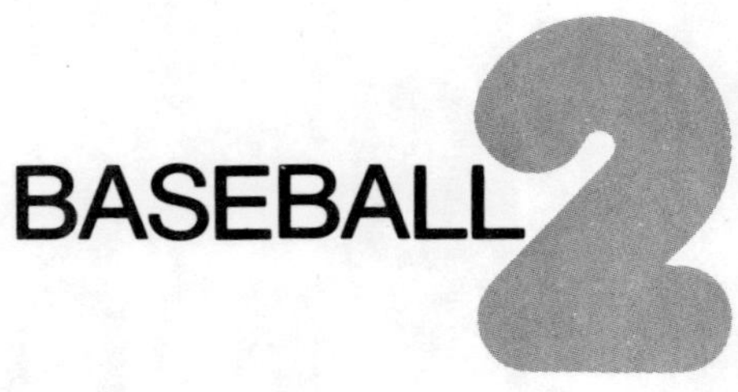

Library of Congress Cataloging in Publication Data
Deegan, Paul J 1937-
Bunting and Baserunning.
SUMMARY: Instructions for the beginning baseball player in bunting and base running techniques.
1. Batting (Baseball)—Juvenile literature. 2. Base Running (Baseball)—Juvenile literature. (1. Batting (Baseball) 2. Base Running (Baseball) 3. Baseball)
I. Henriksen, Harold. II. Title.
GV869.D42 796.357'26 75-15817 ISBN 0-87191-431-X

Library of Congress Number: 75-15817 ISBN: 0-87191-431-X

For Lisa, Mike, and John – may participation in athletics bring you as much enjoyment as it has brought your dad.

The most commonly used bunt is the sacrifice bunt. It is called that because the batter gives up or sacrifices his chance to try for a hit. He uses his time at bat to advance a runner or runners on base.

Any baseball player should be able to learn to bunt. Attitude is perhaps a bigger problem than technique. A player must be willing to sacrifice a chance to hit for the benefit of the team. A batter has to be willing to make an out in order to move a teammate into better scoring position.

When a coach or manager calls for a sacrifice bunt, it's usually a crucial situation. One run is very important at that point in the game. The sacrifice bunt is an act of team loyalty by the batter. Even baseball's scoring system recognizes this — a sacrifice is not counted as an official time at bat.

give yourself up!!!

A player should be able successfully to complete the sacrifice bunt at least six out of every ten times. One major league manager says eight out of ten times.

It is easier to lay down a bunt than to swing for a hit. You don't have to bring a moving bat against a ball in motion when you bunt. You only have to get the bat on the same level as the moving ball.

The best way for young players to lay down a sacrifice bunt is to square around in the batter's box. You don't have to disguise your intention to bunt when you're sacrificing. Start to square around when the pitcher begins his stretch. If you're playing in a league where base runners are not permitted to lead off, square around when the pitcher winds up.

Move your front foot forward and away from the plate — out and to the side. Bring your rear foot up next to the front foot. Make sure you don't place this foot outside the batter's box. If your foot's out of the box and you make contact with the ball, you're out.

Never square around to bunt by pulling your front foot back. You want to bunt the ball when it's out in front of the plate. To do this, you must be well forward in the batter's box. If you're further back, there is less fair territory into which you can bunt the ball.

After you've squared-off your feet, move up your top hand on the bat toward the trademark. Keep your fingers behind the bat; don't wrap them around it. The bottom hand remains down by the knob of the bat.

As the pitch comes to you, push the bat almost straight out in front of you at shoulder level. The bat should be well out in front of the plate. It is important to hold the bat at shoulder level. If you hold the bat lower, you'll have to move it up to bunt pitches high in the strike zone. When you move the bat up to bunt a ball, you're likely to pop the ball in the air. Also, when the bat is held at shoulder level, you know that any pitch above the bat is out of the strike zone. You only want to go after strikes when you're sacrifice-bunting.

If the pitch is lower than bat level, get the bat on the ball by bending at the waist and knees. Keep the bat at shoulder level.

contact ball in front of plate

Make sure you contact the ball in front of the plate. Let the ball meet the bat. Don't push the bat at the ball. The added motion just makes bunting more difficult. Let the ball rebound off the bat.

When you want to soften the bunt, don't pull the bat back. Again this is just extra motion. Instead, loosen your grip on the bat. You might want a softer bunt if the infield is all dirt. When you want to bunt harder, tighten your grip.

Where should you try to bunt the ball?

On a regular baseball field, keep the bunt on the grass portion of the infield. This slows down the ball enough so that no fielder should be able to throw out the base runner whom you're trying to advance.

If there is no grass in the infield, there are only two places you do NOT want the bunt to go. One place is directly back at the pitcher. If the ball goes right to the pitcher, the defense will have a good chance to throw out the advancing runner. The other place you do not want to try to bunt the ball is down the foul lines.

A bunt that hangs just inside a foul line is not the perfect bunt. It's just darn lucky.

If you try to bunt the ball straight down a foul line, you greatly reduce your chances of bunting the ball fair.

The bunter must know that if he or she attempts to bunt when he has two strikes, and misses, it's an out. It is scored as a strikeout.

There are bunts other than the sacrifice. They are the squeeze bunts and the bunt for a hit.

The squeeze bunts are intended to score a runner from third base. The bunter's technique is the same as for the sacrifice. Make sure, though, that you don't give the bunt away before the pitcher has begun throwing to the plate. The squeeze bunt can be directed any place in fair territory except right back at the pitcher.

There is a safety squeeze and a suicide squeeze. On a safety squeeze, the runner does not break for home until he sees that the bunt has been hit on the ground. The batter does not bunt the ball unless it's a strike.

Dodgers
24
suicide
get bat
on the ball!!

The runner moves with the pitch on a suicide squeeze. Therefore the batter must get the bat on the ball somehow, even if the pitch is not in the strike zone. Fouling off a pitch is better than missing the ball. If the batter misses the ball, the runner is usually a sure out.

On a suicide squeeze, the runner and the pitch will arrive at almost the same time. If the catcher has to delay for even a few moments because he doesn't see the runner, the catcher may not be able to make the tag on the runner. Therefore, a right-handed batter should remain in the batter's box if he has been unable to bunt or foul-off the pitcher. By remaining in the box, the batter may be able to screen the catcher's view for a few moments. The batter, however, may not step directly into the catcher's way.

A squeeze bunt is usually commanded by a sign from the base coaches to both batter and runners. It is very important that the batter be required to return a sign when the suicide squeeze has been called. The runner needs to be absolutely sure that the batter knows the squeeze is on. The runner could be injured if the batter swings away as the runner reaches the plate. Returning a sign is called a "recognition sign."

A bunt for a hit succeeds because it's not expected. It must surprise the defense.

Bunting for a hit is a good move at certain times, especially if the batter is a fast runner. The bunt is likely to go for a hit if directed toward a first or third baseman playing very deep. It's also a good bet if the first or third baseman does not throw well.

A left-handed batter has an advantage in bunting for a hit because he is starting from the plate two steps closer to first base.

Whether you bat left-handed or right-handed, you have to disguise your intent to bunt for a hit. You must stay in your normal hitting stance until the pitch is well on its way. If you don't, the first and third basemen can move in quickly and get in position easily to field your bunt.

The first move for a left-handed batter bunting for a hit is a step forward with the left foot. Push the left hand down on the bat at the same time as you step forward. Step toward the pitcher. You will end up facing directly toward first base. You will be able to reach any ball thrown over the plate. Move the bat in front of you to chest height. Make sure the bat is level. Hold the bat still, and let the ball hit the bat.

When the ball hits the bat, a left-handed batter's weight is on his right foot. The bunter then pushes off the right foot to begin the sprint to first base.

The first move for a right-handed batter bunting for a hit is to take a stride backward with the right foot. Shift your weight to the left foot. Slide the right hand down on the bat and move the bat to chest level. Push the barrel of the bat forward so that the front of the bat points toward first base. Hold the bat level and let the ball rebound off it.

As the ball is bunted, shift your weight back to the right foot. Move the left

foot forward and swing the right foot toward first base. Push off the right foot to begin your sprint to first.

Too often a player who has decided to bunt for a hit goes after the pitch, no matter where it's been thrown. It's very difficult to bunt a pitch that's way out of the strike zone. If you're going to try bunting for hits, you must

learn to snap the bat back quickly on a ball out of the strike zone, letting the ball go by.

Probably the most important factor in winning or losing youth league games is baserunning.

All successful base runners do not have great speed. Speed helps, but it's equally important to be alert.

Baserunning begins with the batter going to first base. The first thing young players must learn is NOT TO THROW THE BAT. You don't have to set it down; just drop it. Then go hard for first base. Run as hard as you can. Use good sprinting form. Make sure you RUN IN A STRAIGHT LINE. If you don't, you're wasting time as well as effort.

Baseball rules say you must stay in the running path — the area three-feet to the outside of the first base line — for the last 45 feet before first base. This is the running path on a regulation-sized field with 90 feet between bases.

What the runner does going to first base depends upon whether the ball is likely to be played by an infielder or appears to be going into the outfield.

If the ball was hit on the ground and is likely to be played by an infielder, watch the coach as you approach first. The coach will direct you by both hand signals and shouts to continue to second if the ball has been misplayed.

If the infielder plays the ball and throws to first, don't jump at the base in an effort to beat the throw. You lose foot speed when your feet don't maintain contact with the ground. Jumping slows you down.

Another mistake players often make is taking an extra-long stride to reach the base. This, too, actually slows you down. Stay in stride. Hit the base with either foot. Your stride will determine which foot. Shorten your final stride if necessary.

Once you've touched the base, slow to a stop as quickly as you can. If the ball has been thrown away, you want to be able to continue quickly to second base. After stopping, you may turn in ANY direction. The only thing you may not do is make a break for second. If you do, you can be tagged out. After turning, return to first base. Stay there until you know whether the umpire has called you safe or out.

Sometimes the coach might signal you to continue to second while you're still on your way to first. When this happens, belly out your path to first so you can make as flat a turn as possible over the first base bag. This reduces the distance to second. Round first at full speed, touching the corner of the base closest to the pitcher.

Any time you round first going for second, locate the ball for yourself. Decide yourself whether or not you can safely continue to second. Determine the location of the ball and how it's being handled by the fielders. Weigh these things against your foot speed and how fast the second baseman or shortstop is moving to cover second.

Any time you reach first base, always look for an opportunity to advance safely to second. You can score from second on a single. Generally, you can't from first. If you're on second instead of first, you have also taken away the possibility of a ground-ball double play.

When you hit the ball to the outfield, always make the turn at first at full speed. Do this even if you're sure your fly ball to the outfield is going to be caught.

Once you get to first, make the defense stop you by returning the ball quickly and cleanly to the infield.

Make the most of baserunning. Running is the only thing young players can do as well as older ones on the baseball field. Add some intelligence and common sense to your running, and you will become a real threat.

A good base runner must always be aggressive. You want to take advantage of every opportunity, however small. Aggressive does not mean reckless. There's only a fine line between the two. A good base runner must learn the difference.

Baserunning also involves signals, leading off, stealing, thinking ahead, tagging up, locating the base, and sliding.

Signals or signs are a communications system which is used instead of language. Signs replace language so that the other team doesn't know what your team is going to do.

Signs may be spoken or unspoken. Usually they're unspoken — simple acts such as touching the cap or belt, brushing a hand across a sleeve or the letters of the uniform.

Some teams use an "attention getter." This is a common word, such as a name, or phrase which a coach uses to alert a runner or batter that a sign is coming.

Whether or not your team uses an attention getter, a runner should watch the coach before every pitch to see whether a sign is being given. Don't get in the habit of turning your head away from the coach immediately after you receive a sign. This will help the other team recognize your signs. If you think you missed a sign, call time-out and talk with the coach.

Some of you will play in youth leagues where leading off is not permitted. Even so, you must get your body ready to move off the base after every pitch. Move off the base a few feet when the pitch reaches the plate.

When you play under regular baseball rules, you may lead off. Remember that the purpose of leading off is to cut down the distance you must run to the next base. However, you don't want to get so far off that you can easily be picked off.

How far you should lead off depends upon your own speed and quickness, what base you're at, and the pitcher. You can lead farther from second base than from first. At third base, you can lead farther if the pitcher is winding up rather than throwing from a stretch. You can take a bigger lead at first against a right-handed pitcher than you can against a left-hander.

You must always have your weight under control when you're leading off. Do not put too much weight on the foot farthest from the base. It's when you're leaning in the wrong direction that you're likely to get picked off. Side-step away from the base to keep your weight in balance. Don't cross your feet when you step away from the base. Crouch slightly and keep your weight on the balls of your feet. Don't lean back on your heels. This will freeze you in your steps.

Always lead off directly toward the next base except in two instances. If you're on second with no runner at third, you want to angle a couple steps toward the shortstop. This will give you a flatter turn at third base, cutting down the distance between second and the plate. The other exception is when you're on third base. Here you always lead off in foul territory — outside the third baseline. This is done to avoid being hit in fair territory by a batted ball. If this happens, the runner's out.

Stealing depends upon getting a good jump on the pitch. You can steal successfully without great speed if you can get a good jump. To do this you must know when the pitcher is going to throw to the plate instead of to a base. Study each pitcher's motion. Learn when a pitcher has reached the point in his delivery where he has committed himself to throwing to the plate. Then you can take off.

Stealing will often be done only by a sign from the manager or coach. In leagues where leading off is not permitted, there will probably be no attempts to steal except after a wild pitch or a passed ball.

Older players will sometimes be permitted to decide for themselves when to steal. The runner considering stealing must keep in mind the score, the number of outs, the count, who's batting, and his or her chances of success against a particular pitcher.

When your team is several runs ahead, a steal is usually not worth the risk. If several runs behind, it won't help your team much either. A count of two balls and one strike on the batter is a good time to steal; no balls and two strikes is not a good time.

When you're going to steal, get as good a lead as you can. Keep your weight balanced. Make up your mind to go. As the pitcher reaches the point where he has to

throw to the plate, shift your weight to your front foot, pump your arms and start your legs moving. Then try to get a very quick start.

Stealing third base should be more difficult than stealing second. Even though the base runner can take a longer lead from second, the catcher only has to throw the ball about two-thirds as far to third as to second. It

is not only an easier throw, it gets there much quicker than a throw to second. Sometimes, however, stealing third base is easier than stealing second. This is true when the pitcher is not carefully watching the runner or when the catcher is careless.

The good base runner must always be thinking ahead. Any one of several things might happen on the next pitch. You must know what you will do if there's a wild pitch, a passed ball, or a base hit. The ball may be hit on the ground or in the air. It may be hit to an infielder or deep to the outfield. If you haven't thought ahead of time about what you will do, there won't be enough time after something happens to think about it and react properly.

Making the correct decision means the runner must always know what's going on in the game. The runner must know the number of outs, the count on the batter, how many — if any — runners are also on base, and the importance of the run he represents.

When you're on first base, you'll always be forced to run on a ground ball. Move quickly to second and slide hard. You may be able to break-up a double play attempt.

If you're on second or third and not forced to run, you have to know the importance of the run you represent. You must decide how much of a chance to take.

Runners must also learn whether or not they should tag up on fly balls to the outfield when there are fewer than two outs. Runners never tag up when there are two outs. They go hard to the next base as soon as the ball is hit.

To tag up, position yourself so that you can see when the fielder touches the fly ball. You may run as soon as the ball is touched.

When you're at first base and a fly ball is hit to the outfield, don't tag up except in two instances. Tag up if a fly ball is hit very deep to the outfield and it appears that the ball will be caught. You might be able to advance to second after the catch. Also tag up at first on any fly ball to the outfield IF there's also a runner at third base. You do this so that you can advance to second if the throw from the outfield goes to the plate.

When you're on second, tag up if the ball's hit to center or right field and it looks as though the ball will be caught. You may be able to advance to third after the catch.

The runner at third base ALWAYS tags up on a fly ball to the outfield when there are fewer than two out. Tag up no matter what. You can score easily if the ball falls for a hit or is misplayed. If the ball is hit fairly deep and caught, and you're several feet off the bag, you've given up an easy chance to score. Remember — base runners may also tag up and advance after a fly ball is caught in foul territory. Take advantage of this when you can.

Base runners must be aware of the infield fly rule. This rule applies when there are fewer than two out. If in the opinion of the umpire a fly ball can be fielded by an infielder, the batter is automatically out. Runners advance at their own risk.

A runner should coach himself when he is on base and the ball is hit to his right. This puts the ball in front of him where he can see how it is being played. When the ball is hit to the base runner's left or behind him, the runner must depend upon a coach's shouts or signals in determining what to do.

Going into second or third base, a coach should let the runner know whether to slide or stand up. Going into third base, even if the coach stops you, you must locate the ball immediately. If the ball gets by the catcher or whoever is covering the plate, the runner is the only one who can react fast enough to score.

A runner going to the plate should know that there's now a third coach on the field. The third coach is the on-deck hitter, the player next up to bat. Since a play at the plate is usually a tag play, the on-deck hitter must signal the runner to slide or stay up. The on-deck hitter must position himself so that the runner can easily see him. The correct position for the on-deck hitter is directly on a line with the third base line, a few feet back from the plate.

Learning to slide correctly makes you a better base runner. It may also someday save you from a broken leg. Sliding usually comes easily to young players. It is not difficult, but it does require some courage because, simply put, you're just throwing yourself on the ground.

The purpose of a slide is to stop at a base without overrunning it, and, on a close play, to avoid a tag or make the tag difficult. Sometimes a slide may even jar the ball from a fielder's hand.

Young ballplayers should use the straight-in slide. When they get older, they can work on a pop-up slide, a hook slide, and a head-first slide. The head-first slide can be dangerous unless the slider has confidence in what he's doing.

Sliding is a controlled fall. You want to contact the ground with as much of your body as possible. This spreads the shock of the impact of hitting the ground over the legs, hips, and, sometimes, even the back.

When you fall to slide, keep your hands well off the ground to avoid injuring them. Throw back the upper part of your body. Keep your feet off the ground as well as your hands. You do not want to catch your spikes in the dirt and possibly injure an ankle.

You can practice sliding by yourself. If possible, get hold of a base and stake it down on a grassy area. Make sure you're wearing long pants. Practice sliding into the base. If you have no base, use a piece of cardboard.

You can also practice sliding on a gym floor if you wear a sweat shirt and sweat pants. To avoid floor burns, pull the shirt sleeves over your hands. Take off your shoes and pull the pants over your feet. You'll really go fast because there is so little friction. Therefore, when you go out on a baseball field, where you will slide slower, remember

not to begin your slide too soon.

Knowing the correct things to do, developing them through experience in practice and games can make you a good base runner. Remember, great speed is not required if you know the situation, think ahead about what might happen, and react with common sense.

BASEBALL
pitching
hitting
bunting and baserunning

FOOTBALL
passing the football
catching the football
placekicking and punting

BASKETBALL
the set shot
the jump shot
shooting in a game

TENNIS
the basic strokes
serving and returning service
volleying and lobs

HOCKEY
skates and sticks
stickhandling and passing
shooting
checking and defensive play

creative
education
sports
instructional
series for
young
people